Al-Fuyudat al-Rabbaniyya (Emanations of Lordly Grace)

Shaikh Abdul Qadir Jilani
(May Allah be pleased with him)

Translated By:

Shaikh Muhammad ibn Yahya at-Tadifi al-Hanbalion

KITAB BHAVAN
New Delhi - 110 002 (INDIA)

Name of the Book	: Al-Fuyudat al-Rabbaniya (Emanations of Lordly Grace)
Written by	: Shaikh Abdul Qadir Jilani
Translated by	: Shaikh Muhammad ibn Yahya at-Tadifi al-Hanbalion
Reprint	: 2019
ISBN-10	: 81-7151-389-1
ISBN-13	: 978-81-7151-389-5
Book Code No.	: A00079

Printed & Published in India by : Moonis Ali Nasri for KITAB BHAVAN
1784, Kalan Mahal, Darya Ganj,
New Delhi - 1100 02 [India]

PRINTED IN INDIA

If you have any corrections, comments. or questions about this publication, please feel free to contact us.

CONTENTS

CONTENTS

ya bahru bi-la taraf.

O Gray Falcon!
ya Bazu'l-Ashhab.

O reliever of sorrows!
ya farija'l-kurab.

O Helper Supreme!
ya Ghawthu'l-A'zam.

O abundant source of kindness and generosity!
ya wasi'a'l-lutfi wa'l-karam.

O treasury of the realities!
ya kanza'l-haqa'iq.

O mine of the subtleties!
ya ma'dina'd-daqa'iq.

O means of order and progress!
ya wasita's-silki wa's-suluk.

O master of kingship and the kings!
ya sahiba'l-mulki wa'l-muluk.

O sun of suns!
ya shamsa'sh-shumus.

O flower of the souls!
ya zahrata'n-nufus.

O blower of the fragrant breeze!
ya hawiya'n-nasim.

O reviver of the decayed!

ya muhyiya'r-ramim.

O lofty of aspiration!
ya 'aliya'l-hamim.

O law of the nations!
ya namusa'l-umam.

O proof of the ardent lovers!
ya hujjata'l-'ashiqin.

O scion of the family of Ta-Ha and Ya-Sin.
ya Sulalata ali Ta-Ha wa Ya-Sin.

O Sultan of those who reach their goal!
ya Sultana'l-wasilin.

O heir of the Selected Prophet!
ya waritha'n-Nabiyyi'l-Mukhtar.

O vault of the mysteries!
ya khizanata'l-asrar.

O displayer of the Beauty of Allah!
ya mubdiya Jamali'llah.

O deputy of Allah's Messenger!
ya na'iba Rasuli'llah.

O heart of the Chosen!
ya kabida'l-Mustafa.

O master of fidelity!
ya sahiba'l-wafa.

O secret of the Preferred!

ya sirra'l-Mujtaba.

O light of the Approved!
ya nur al-Murtada.

O consolation of the eyes!
ya qurrata'l-'uyun.

O possessor of the blessed face!
ya dha'l-wajhi'l-maimun.

O sound in spiritual states!
ya saliha'l-ahwal.

O truthful in utterances!
ya sadiqa'l-aqwal.

O unsheathed sword of Allah!
ya saifa'llahi'l-maslul.

O fruit of the purely devoted lady [Fatima]!
ya thamarata'l-batul.

O sympathizer with the people!
ya rahima'n-nas.

O remover of injury!
ya mudhhiba'l-bas.

O opener of treasures!
ya mufattiha'l-kunuz.

O source of secret signs!
ya ma'dina'r-rumuz.

O Ka'ba of those who reach their destination!

ya Ka'bata'l-wasilin.

O means of connection for the seekers!
ya wasilata't-talibin.

O shedder of luxuriant rain!
ya mukhjila'l-matar.

O benefactor of the human being!
ya muhsina'l-bashar.

O strength of the weak!
ya quwwata'd-du'afa'.

O refuge of the strangers!
ya malja'a'l-ghuraba'.

O leader of the devout!
ya imama'l-muttaqin.

O best of the worshipful servants!
ya safwata'l-'abidin.

O strong one of the pillars!
ya qawiyya'l-arkan.

O beloved friend of the All-Merciful!
ya habiba'r-Rahman.

O revealer of the Eternally Pre-existent Speech!
ya mujliya'l-Kalami'l-Qadim.

O healing of the ailments of the sick!
ya shifa'a asqami's-saqim.

O most righteous of the righteous!

ya atqa'l-atqiya'.

O purest of the pure!
ya asfa'l-asfiya'.

O kindled Fire of Allah!
ya Nara'llahi'l-muqada.

O life of the hearts!
ya hayata'l-af'ida.

O Shaikh of all!
ya Shaikha'l-kull.

O guide of the ways!
ya dalila's-subul.

O chieftain of the loved ones!
ya naqiba'l-mahbubin.

O destination of the spiritual travellers!
ya maqsuda's-salikin.

O noble on both sides [of the family]!
ya karima't-tarafain.

O pillar of both parties!
ya 'umdata'l-fariqain.

O judge of the judges!
ya qadiya'l-qudat.

O opener of the doors that are locked!
ya fatiha'l-mughlaqat.

O sufficient supplier of important provisions!

ya kafiya'l-muhimmat.

O wall surrounding all things!
ya ha'ita'l-ashya'.

O light of the council!
ya nura'l-mala'.

O fulfilment of hope when the work is done!
ya muntaha'l-amali hina yanqati'u'l-'amal.

O chief of the chiefs!
ya sayyida's-sadat.

O source of felicity!
ya manba'a's-sa'adat.

O light of the heavens and the earths!
ya diya'a's-samawati wa'l-aradin.

O dictionary of the preachers!
ya qamusa'l-wa'izin.

O eye of humankind!
ya 'aina'l-wara.

O guide of those who travel by night!
ya qudwata's-sura.

O abundance of benefits!
ya jamma'l-fawa'id.

O relief in adversities!
ya farajan fi'sh-shada'id.

O ocean of the Sacred Law!

ya bahra'sh-Shari'a.

O Sultan of the Spiritual Path!
ya Sultana't-Tariqa.

O proof of Reality!
ya burhana'l—Haqiqa.

O interpreter of the knowledge of experience!
ya tarjumana'l-Ma'rifa.

O discloser of secrets!
ya kashifa'l-asrar.

O forgiver of transgressions!
ya ghafira'l-awzar.

O model of the saints!
ya tiraza'l-awliya'.

O support of the poor!
ya 'aduda'l-fuqara'.

O master of splendid spiritual states!
ya dha'l-ahwali'l-'azima.

O master of compassionate qualities!
ya dha'l-awsafi'r-rahima.

O master of the clear religion!
ya dha'l-millati'l-jaliyya.

O master of the Hanbali school [of Islamic law]!
ya dha'l-madhhabi'l-Hanbaliyya.

O leader of the leaders!

ya imama'l-a'imma.

O remover of distress!
ya kashifa'l-ghumma.

O solver of difficult problems!
ya fatiha'l-mushkilat.

O welcome guest of the Lord of the Gardens [of Paradise]!
ya maqbulu Rabbi'l-Jannat.

O boon companion of the All-Merciful!
ya jalisa'r-Rahman.

O famous native of Jilan!
ya mashhuran mina'l-Jilan.

O Emperor!
ya Shah.

O secret of my God!
ya sirra Ilahi.

O virtuous one!
ya 'afif.

O noble one!
ya sharif.

O dutifully devoted one!
ya taqi.

O pure one!
ya naqi.

O champion of the Truth!

ya Siddiq.

O ardently beloved!
ya Ma'shuq.

O Cardinal Pole of the cardinal poles!
ya Qutba'l-aqtab.

O uniquely beloved!
ya farda'l-ahbab.

O my master!
ya sayyidi

O my support!
ya sanadi.

O my patron!
ya mawlaya.

O my strength!
ya quwwati.

O my helper!
ya ghawthi.

O my aid!
ya ghiyathi.

O my assistant!
ya 'awni.

O my comfort!
ya rahati.

O satisfier of my needs!

ya qadiya hajati.

O dispeller of my sorrow!
ya farija karbati.

O my radiance!
ya diya'i.

O my hope!
ya raja'i.

O my remedy!
ya shifa'i.

O Sultan Muhyi'd-Din 'Abd al-Qadir!
ya Sultanu Muhyi'd-Dini 'Abdi'l-Qadir.

O light of the innermost beings!
ya nura's-sara'ir.

O possessor of power!
ya sahiba'l-qudra.

O bestower of glory!
ya qahiba'l-'azama.

O He whose secret is manifest in this world and the Hereafter!
ya man zahara sirru-hu fi'd-dunya wa'l-akhira.

O king of the age!
ya malika'z-zaman.

O He who carries out the commandment of Allah!
ya man yuqimu bi-amri'llah.

O inheritor of the Book of Allah!

ya waritha Kitabi'llah.

O inheritor of the Messenger of Allah!
ya waritha Rasuli'llah.

O Cardinal Pole of the cardinal poles!
ya Qutba'l-aqtab.

O presence of Shaikh 'Abd al-Qadir
ya hadrata'sh-Shaikh 'Abdi'l-Qadir

(may Allah sanctify his innermost being and illuminate his mausoleum)!
(qaddasa'llahu sirra-hu wa nawwir dariha-h)

O secret of secrets!
ya sirra'l-asrar.

O Ka'ba of the righteous!
ya Ka'bata'l-abrar.

O Shaikh of every Cardinal Pole and Helper!
ya Shaikha kulli Qutbin wa Ghawth.

O witness of all beings at a glance!
ya shahida'l-akwani bi-nazra.

O observer of the Throne through his knowledge!
ya mubsira'l-'Arshi bi-'ilmi-h.

O traveller to the east and the west with a single step!
ya baligha'l-gharbi wa'sh-sharqi bi-khatwa.

O Cardinal Pole of the angels, the human race and the jinn!
ya Qutba'l-mala'ikati wa'l-insi wa'l-jinn.

O Cardinal Pole of the land and the sea!

ya Qutba'l-barri wa'l-bahr.

O Cardinal Pole of the east and the west!
ya Qutba'l-mashriqi wa'l-maghrib.

O Cardinal Pole of the heavens and the earths!
ya Qutba's-samawati wa'l-aradin.

O Cardinal Pole of the Throne and the Pedestal,
ya Qutba'l-'Arshi wa'l-Kursiyyi

and of the Tablet and the Pen!
wa'l-Lawhi wa'l-Qalam.

O master of aspiration and of intercession!
ya sahiba'l-himma wa'sh-shafa'a.

O He who reaches his disciple when the appeal for help is made,
ya man yablughu li-muridi-hi 'inda'l-istighatha:

even if he is [far away] in the east!
wa law kana fi'l-mashriq.

Your horse is saddled and your sword is unsheathed;
farasu-ka masrujatun wa saifu-ka maslulun

your spear is raised and your bow is strung;
wa rumhu-ka mansubun wa qawsu-ka mawturun

your arrow is on target and your mount is ready to ride!
wa sahmu-ka sa'ibun wa rikabu-ka'al.

O master of generosity and noble grace!
ya Sahiba'l-judi wa'l-karam.

O master of the fine traits of character and aspirations!

ya sahiba'l-akhlaqi'l-hasanati wa'l-himam.

O master of dispensation in this world,
ya sahiba't-tasarrufi fi'd-dunya

and in his grave, by Allah's leave!
wa fi qabri-hi bi-idhni'llah.

O master of the foot raised over the neck of every saint of Allah!
ya sahiba'l-qadami'l-'ali 'ala raqabati kulli waliyyin li'llah.

O Supreme Helper, help me in all my states,
ya Ghawthu'l-A'zamu aghith-ni fi kulli ahwali

and support me in all my hopes, and direct me in your path,
wa'nsur-ni fi kulli amali wa taqallab-ni fi tariqi-ka

in honour of your forefather Muhammad
bi-hurmati jaddi-ka Muhammadin

(Allah bless him and give him peace),
(salla'llahu 'alai-hi wa sallam)

and through his intercession, his spirit and his innermost being.
wa bi-shifa'ati-hi wa ruhi-hi wa sirri-h.

May Allah bless our master Muhammad and his family
wa salla'llahu 'ala sayyidi-na Muhammadin wa 'ala ali-hi

and his Companions, and may He grant them peace.
wa sahbi-hi wa sallam.

There is no power nor any strength
wa la hawla wa la quwwata

except with Allah, the All-High, the Almighty.
illa bi'llahi'l-'Aliyyi'l-'Azim.

THE GHAWTHIYYA
Received By Way Of Heart-Inspiration [Ilham Qalbi] And Spiritual Disclosure [Kashf Ma'nawi]

In the Name of Allah, the All-Merciful, the All-Compassionate.
Bismi'llahi'r-Rahmani'r-Rahim.

Praise be to Allah, the Remover of distress,
al-hamdu li'llahi Kashifi'l-ghumma:

and blessings upon the best of human creatures.
wa's-salawatu 'ala khairi'l-bariyya.

Well then, it was the Supreme Helper, he who was estranged
qala'l-Ghawthu'l-A'zamu'l-mustawhishu

from all apart from Allah, but intimately friendly with Allah, who said:
'an ghairi'llahi wa'l-musta'nisu bi'llah:

Allah (Exalted is He) said: "O Supreme Helper!"
qala'llahu (ta'ala) ya Ghawtha'l-A'zam:

I replied: "Doubly [outwardly and inwardly] at your service,
qultu labbaika

O Lord of the Helper!
ya Rabba'l-Ghawth.

He said: "Every stage between the Realm of Humanity
qala kullu tawrin baina'n-Nasuti

and the Realm of Sovereignty is a Sacred Law.
wa'l-Malakuti fa-huwa Shari'a:

Every stage between the Realm of Sovereignty

wa kullu tawrin baina'l-Malakuti

and the Realm of Dominion is a Spiritual Path
wa'l-Jabaruti fa-huwa Tariqa:

Every stage between the Realm of Dominion
wa kullu tawrin baina'l-Jabaruti

and the Realm of Divinity is a Reality
wa'l-Lahuti fa-huwa Haqiqa."

Then He said to me: "O Supreme Helper,
thumma qala li ya Ghawthu'l-A'zamu

I have not manifested Myself in anything
ma zahartu fi shai'in

like My Self-manifestation in the human being."
ma zahartu fi shai'in ka-zuhuri fi'l-insan.

Then I asked: "O my Lord, do you have a location?"
thumma sa'altu ya Rabbi hal la-ka makan.

He said to me: "O Supreme Helper,
qala li ya Ghawthu'l-A'zamu

I am the Creator of location, and I have no location."
Ana Mukawwinu'l-makani wa laisa li makan.

Then I asked: "O my Lord, do You have food and drink?"
thumma sa'altu ya Rabbi hal la-ka aklun wa shurb.

He said to me: "O Supreme Helper,
qala li ya Ghawthu'l-A'zamu

the food and drink of the pauper are My food and drink."
aklu'l-faqir wa shurbu-hu akli wa shurbi.

Then I asked: "O my Lord, from what thing did You create the angels?"
thumma sa'altu ya Rabbi min ayyi shai'in khalaqta'l-mala'ika.

He said to me: "O Supreme Helper,
qala li ya Ghawthu'l-A'zamu

I created the angels from the light of the human being,
khalaqtu'l-mala'ikata min nuri'l-insani

and I created the human being from My Light."
wa khalaqtu'l-insana min nuri.

Then He said to me: "O Supreme Helper,
thumma qala li ya Ghawthu'l-A'zamu

I have made the human being My riding animal,
ja'altu'l-insana matiyyati

and I have made the rest of the universe a riding animal for him."
wa ja'altu sa'ira'l-akwan matiyyatan la-h.

Then He said to me: "O Supreme Helper,
thumma qala li ya Ghawthu'l-A'zamu

what an excellent Seeker am I!
ni'ma't-Talibu Ana

What an excellent object to be sought is the human being!
wa ni'ma'l-matlubu'l-insan:

What an excellent rider is the human being,
wa ni'ma'r-rakibu'l-insan:

and what an excellent means of transport are the entities of the universe!"
wa ni'ma'l-markubu la-hu'l-akwan.

Then He said to me: "O Supreme Helper, the human being
thumma qala li ya Ghawthu'l-A'zamu'l-insanu

is My secret, and I am his secret. If the human being was truly aware
sirri wa Ana sirru-hu law'arafa'l-insanu

of his situation in My sight, he would say, with every single breath:
manzilata-hu'indi la-qala fi kulli nafasin min al-anfasi

'To whom does the supreme authority belong today?'"
li-mani'l-mulku'l-yawm.

Then He said to me: "O Supreme Helper, the human being
thumma qala li ya Ghawthu'l-A'zamu ma akala'l-insanu

does not eat anything, nor does he drink, nor does he stand,
shai'an wa ma shariba shai'an wa ma qama

nor does he sit, nor does he speak, nor does he keep silent,
wa ma qa'ada wa ma nataqa wa ma samata

nor does he do any deed, nor does he turn toward anything,
wa ma fa'ala fi'lan wa ma tawajjaha li-shai'in

nor does he move away from anything, except that I am in him,
wa ma ghaba'an shai'in illa wa Ana fi-hi

dwelling within him and causing him to move."
sakinu-hu wa mutaharriku-h.

Then He said to me: "O Supreme Helper,
thumma qala li ya Ghawthu'l-A'zamu

the physical body of the human being, his instinctive self, his heart,
jismu'l-insani wa nafsu-hu wa qalbu-hu

his spirit, his hearing, his sight, his hand, his foot, and his tongue –
wa ruhu-hu wa sam'u-hū wa basaru-hu wa yadu-hu wa rijlu-hu wa lisanu-hu

all of that I have presented to him by Myself, for Myself.
wa kullu dhalika azhartu la-hu bi-Nafsi li-Nafsi

It is nothing other than I, and I am not other than it."
la huwa illa Ana wa la Ana ghairu-h.

Then He said to me: "O Supreme Helper,
thumma qala li ya Ghawthu'l-A'zamu

when you see someone burning in the fire of poverty,
idha ra'aita'l-muhtariqa bi-nari'l-faqri

and devastated by the enormity of need, you must draw close to him,
wa'l-munkasira bi-kathrati'l-faqati fa-taqarrab ilai-hi

because there is no barrier between Me and him."
li-anna-hu la hijaba baini wa baina-h.

Then He said to me: "O Supreme Helper,
thumma qala li ya Ghawthu'l-A'zamu

you must not eat any food, nor drink any drink,
la ta'kul ta'aman wa la tashrab sharaban

nor sleep a wink of sleep, except in the presence
wa la tanam nawmatan illa'inda

of a heart that is fully aware, and of an eye that is watching.
qalbin hadirin wa'ainin nazir.

Then He said to me: "O Supreme Helper,
thumma qala li ya Ghawthu'l-A'zamu

if someone is excluded from My journey in the inner, he will be tried
man hurima'an safari fi'l-batini'btuliya

with the outer journey, and he will receive no provision from Me,
bi-safari'z-zahiri wa lam yazdad min-ni

except distance in the outer journey."
illa bu'dan fi safari'l-batin.

Then He said to me: "O Supreme Helper, spiritual coalition is a state
thumma qala li ya Ghawthu'l-A'zamu'l-ittihadu halun

that cannot be expressed by the tongue of speech.
la yu'abbaru bi-lisani'l-maqali

If someone professes belief therein,
fa-man amana bi-hi

before experiencing the existence of the state, he is guilty of unbelief.
qabla wujudi'l-hali fa-qad kafara

If someone wishes to practice formal worship after the attainment of direct contact,
wa man arada'l-'ibadata ba'da'l-wusuli

he is guilty of attributing partners to Allah the Almighty."
fa-qad ashraka bi'llahi'l-'Azim.

Then He said to me: "O Supreme Helper, if someone is blessed
thumma qala li ya Ghawthu'l-A'zamu

with the good fortune of eternity-without-beginning,
man sa'ida bi's-sa'adati'l-azaliyyati

congratulations are due to him! He will never be disappointed.
tuba la-hu lam yakun makhdhulan abada:

If someone must suffer the misfortune of eternity-without-beginning,
wa man shaqa bi'sh-shaqawati'l-azaliyyati

woe unto him! He will never be accepted after that."
fa-wailun la-hu lam yakun maqbulan ba'da dhalika qatt.

Then He said to me: "O Supreme Helper,
thumma qala li ya Ghawthu'l-A'zamu

I have made poverty and need the means of transport for the human being.
ja'altu'l-faqra wa'l-faqata matiyyata'l-insani

If someone rides on them, he will surely reach the camp site,
fa-man rakiba-ha fa-qad balagha'l-manzila

before crossing the wastelands and the deserts."
qabla an yaqta'a'l-mafawiza wa'l-bawadi.

Then He said to me: "O Supreme Helper, if the human being
thumma qala li ya Ghawthu'l-A'zamu law'alima'l-insanu

knew what is after death, he would not wish for life in this world.
ma kana ba'da'l-mawti ma tamanna'l-hayata fi'd-dunya

Before each moment and every instant, he would say:
wa yaqulu baina yadai kulli lahzatin wa lamhatin

'O my Lord, cause me to die!'"
ya Rabbi amit-ni.

Then He said to me: "O Supreme Helper,
thumma qala li ya Ghawthu'l-A'zamu

creatures will be confounded in my presence
hujjatu'l-khala'iqi'indi Yawma'l-Qiyamati's-summu'l bukmu'l-'umyu

on the Day of Resurrection, the deaf, the dumb and the blind.
thumma't-tahassuru wa'l-buka'u

Then there will be distress and weeping, and in the grave it will be likewise."
wa fi'l-qabri ka-dhalik.

Then He said to me: "O Supreme Helper, love is a veil
thumma qala li ya Ghawthu'l-A'zamu'l-mahabbatu hijabun

between the lover and the Beloved,
baina'l-muhibbi wa'l-mahbubi

so when the lover becomes extinct to love,
fa-idha faniya'l-muhibbu'an al-mahabbati

he will come in contact with the Beloved."
wasala bi'l-mahbub.

Then He said to me: "O Supreme Helper,
thumma qala li ya Ghawthu'l-A'zamu

I have seen the spirits waiting inside their physical forms,
ra'aitu'l-arwaha yatarabbasuna fi qawalibi-him

after His saying: 'Am I not your Lord?' – until the Day of Resurrection."
ba'da qawli-hi a-lastu bi-Rabbi-kum ila Yawmi'l-Qiyama.

Then the Helper said: "I saw the Lord (Exalted is He),
thumma qala'l-Ghawthu ra'aitu'r-Rabba (ta'ala)

and He said to me: 'O Supreme Helper,
wa qala li ya Ghawthu'l-A'zamu

if someone asks Me about the vision after the knowledge,
man sa'ala-ni'ani'r-ru'yati ba'da'l-'ilmi

he is veiled by the knowledge of the vision.
fa-huwa mahjubun bi-'ilmi'r-ru'ya:

If someone supposes that the vision is other than the knowledge,
fa-man zanna anna'r-ru'yata ghairu'l-'ilmi

he is bedazzled by the vision of Allah (Exalted is He)."
fa-huwa maghrurun bi-ru'yati'llahi (ta'ala).

"Then He said to me: 'O Supreme Helper,
thumma qala li ya Ghawthu'l-A'zamu

if someone sees Me, he is relieved of the need to ask, in every situation.
man ra'a-ni'staghna'ani's-su'ali fi kulli hal:

If someone does not see Me, asking is of no avail to him,
wa man lam yara-ni fa-la yanfa'u-hu's-su'al:

for he is veiled by the act of speech.'"
wa huwa mahjubun bi'l-maqal.

"Then He said to me: 'O Supreme Helper,
thumma qala li ya Ghawthu'l-A'zamu

the pauper in My sight is not someone who has nothing.
laisa'l-faqiru'indi man laisa la-hu shai':

No, the pauper is he who has a power of command in everything,
bali'l-faqiru'lladhi la-hu amrun fi kulli shai':

so that, when he says to a thing, "Be!" it comes into being.'"
idha qala li-shai'in kun fa-yakun.

"Then He said to me: 'There is no friendship and no bliss
thumma qala li la ulfata wa la ni'mata

in the Gardens [of Paradise] after My appearance in them,
fi'l-jinani ba'da zuhuri fi-ha

and there is no loneliness and no burning torment
wa la wahshata wa la hurqata

in the Fire [of Hell] after My address to its inhabitants.'"
fi'n-nari ba'da khitabi li-ahli-ha.

"Then He said to me: 'O Supreme Helper,
thumma qala li ya Ghawthu'l-A'zamu

I am More Generous than any generous person,
Ana Akramu min kulli karim:

and I am More Merciful than any merciful person.'"
wa Ana Arhamu min kulli rahim.

"Then He said to me: 'O Supreme Helper,
thumma qala li ya Ghawthu'l-A'zamu

you must sleep in My presence, not as the common folk sleep,
nam'indi la ka-nawmi'l-'awammi

for then you will see Me.'"
tara-ni.

"To this I replied: 'O my Lord, how should I sleep in Your presence?"
fa-qultu ya Rabbi kaifa anamu'inda-k.

"He said: 'With utter detachment of the body from pleasures,
qala bi-khumudi'l-jismi'ani'l-ladhdhat:

with utter detachment of the self from the desires of the flesh,
wa khumudi'n-nafsi'ani'sh-shahawat:

with utter detachment of the heart from thoughts and emotions,
wa khumudi'l-qalbi ani'l-khatarat:

with utter detachment of the spirit from all distracting glances,
wa khumudi'r-ruhi ani'l-lahazat:

and with the extinction of your essence in the Essence."
wa fana'i dhati-ka fi'dh-Dhat.

"Then He said to me: 'O Supreme Helper,
thumma qala li ya Ghawthu'l-A'zamu

you must tell your companions and your friends [that I say]:
qul li-ashabi-ka wa ahbabi-ka

"If anyone among you wishes for My close presence,
man arada min-kum janabi

it is incumbent upon him to choose poverty, then the poverty of poverty.
fa-'alai-hi bi-'khtiyari'l-faqr: thumma faqri'l-faqr:

Once that poverty is complete, there will be nothing there but I.'"
fa-idha tamma'l-faqru fa-la thamma illa Ana.

"Then He said to me: 'O Supreme Helper,
thumma qala li ya Ghawthu'l-A'zamu

congratulations are due to you, if you are kind to My creatures,
tuba la-ka in kunta ra'ufan'ala bariyyati

and congratulations are due to you, if you are forgiving to My creatures!'"
wa tuba la-ka in kunta ghafuran li-bariyyati.

"Then He said to me: 'O Supreme Helper,
thumma qala li ya Ghawthu'l-A'zamu

tell your friends and your companions [that I say]:
qul li-ahbabi-ka wa ashabi-ka'ghtanimu

"You must seize the appeal of the paupers as an opportunity,
da'wata'l-fuqara'i

for they are with Me, and I am with them.'"
fa-inna-hum'indi wa Ana'inda-hum.

"Then He said to me: 'O Supreme Helper,
thumma qala li ya Ghawthu'l-A'zamu

I am the refuge of every single thing, and its dwelling
Ana ma'wa kulli shai'in wa maskanu-hu

and its watchtower, and to Me is the homeward journey."
wa manzaru-hu wa ilayya'l-masir.

"Then He said to me: 'O Supreme Helper,
thumma qala li ya Ghawthu'l-A'zamu

do not look toward the Garden [of Paradise] and what it contains,
la tanzur ila'l-Jannati wa ma fi-ha

for you can see Me without indirect means.
tara-ni bi-la wasita:

Do not look toward the Fire [of Hell] and what it contains,
wa la tanzur ila'n-Nari wa ma fi-ha

for you can see Me without indirect means".
tara-ni bi-la wasita.

"Then He said to me: 'O Supreme Helper,
thumma qala li ya Ghawthu'l-A'zamu

the people of the Garden [of Paradise] are preoccupied with the Garden, ahlu'l-Jannati mashghuluna bi'l-Jannati

and the people of the Fire [of Hell] are preoccupied with Me.'"
wa ahlu'n-Nari mashghuluna bi.

"Then He said to me: 'O Supreme Helper,
thumma qala li ya Ghawthu'l-A'zamu

some of the people of the Garden [of Paradise] will be seeking refuge
ba'du ahli'l-Jannati yata'awwadhuna

from the sheer bliss, just as the people of the Fire [of Hell]
mina'n-na'im: ka-ahli'n-Nari

will be seeking refuge from the scorching heat."
yata'awwadhuna mina'l-jahim.

"Then He said to me: 'O Supreme Helper,
thumma qala li ya Ghawthu'l-A'zamu

if someone is preoccupied with anything apart from Me, his companion
man shughila bi-siwa'i kana li-sahibi-hi

will be wearing an infidel's girdle on the Day of Resurrection.'"
zunnaran Yawma'l-Qiyama.

"Then He said to me: 'O Supreme Helper,
thumma qala li ya Ghawthu'l-A'zamu

the people of nearness seek help from nearness,
ahlu'l-qurbati yastaghithuna mina'l-qurba:

just as the people of remoteness seek help from remoteness.'"
ka-ma anna ahla'l-bu'di yastaghithuna mina'l-bu'd.

"Then He said to me: 'O Supreme Helper,

thumma qala li ya Ghawthu'l-A'zamu

I have certain servants, apart from the Prophets and the Messengers,
inna li'ibadan siwa'l-Anbiya'i wa'l-Mursalin:

whose spiritual states are not detected by anyone among the people
la yattali'u'ala ahwali-him ahadun min ahli'd-dunya

of this world, nor by anyone among the people of the Hereafter,
wa la ahadun min ahli'l-akhira:

nor by anyone among the people of the Garden [of Paradise],
wa la ahadun min ahli'l-Jannati

nor by anyone among the people of the Fire [of Hell],
wa la ahadun min ahli'n-Nar:

nor by [the angel] Malik, nor by [the angel] Ridwan.
wa la Malikun wa la Ridwan:

I have not assigned them to the Garden, nor to the Fire,
wa la ja'altu-hum li'l-Jannati wa la li'n-Nari

nor to reward, nor to punishment, nor to the fair maids of Paradise,
wa la li'th-thawabi wa la li'l-'iqabi wa la li'l-huri

nor to its palatial mansions, nor to its youthful attendants.
wa la li'l-qusuri wa la li'l-ghilman:

Congratulations, therefore, to anyone who believes in them,
fa-tuba li-man amana bi-him

even if he fails to recognize them!'"
wa in lam ya'rif-hum.

"Then He said to me: 'O Supreme Helper, you are one of them,
thumma qala li ya Ghawthu'l-A'zamu anta min-hum

and their distinctive features in this world include the facts
wa min'alamati-him fi'd-dunya

that their bodies are scorched by the paucity of their food and drink,
ajsamu-hum muhtariqatun min qillati't-ta'ami wa'sh-sharab:

that their lower selves are scorched by their abstinence from carnal desires,
wa nufusu-hum muhtariqatun'ani'sh-shahawat:

that their hearts are scorched by their rejection of thoughts and emotions,
wa qulubu-hum muhtariqatun'ani'l-khatarat:

and that their spirits are scorched by their shunning of distracting glances,
wa arwahu-hum muhtariqatun'ani'l-lahazat:

for they are the owners of perpetuity, scorched
wa hum ashabu'l-baqa'i'l-muhtariqina

by the radiant light of the Meeting [with their Lord].'"
bi-nuri'l-liqa'.

"Then He said to me: 'O Supreme Helper, if a thirsty person
thumma qala li ya Ghawthu'l-A'zamu idha ja'a-ka'atshanun

were ever to approach you, on a day of fierce heat, while you
fi yawmin shadidi'l-harri wa anta

were in possession of cold water, and you were not in need of water,
sahibu'l-ma'i'l-baridi wa laisa la-ka hajatun bi'l-ma':

and if you were to withhold it from him, you would be
fa-law kunta tamna'u-hu fa-anta

the most miserly of all misers. How could I deprive them

abkhalu'l-bakhilin: fa-kaifa amna'u-hum

of My merciful compassion, when I have set the seal upon Myself,
min rahmati wa Ana sajjaltu'ala Nafsi

declaring that I am the Most Merciful of the merciful?'"
bi-anni Arhamu'r-rahimin.

"Then He said to me: 'O Supreme Helper,
thumma qala li ya Ghawthu'l-A'zamu

there is no one, among those guilty of acts of sinful disobedience,
ma ba'uda'an-ni ahadun min ahli'l-ma'asi

who stays away from Me, and there is no one who draws close to Me,
wa ma qaruba ahadun min-ni

among those performing acts of worshipful obedience.'"
min ahli't-ta'at.

"Then He said to me: 'O Supreme Helper,
thumma qala li ya Ghawthu'l-A'zamu

if anyone were to draw close to Me, he would have to be one of those
law qaruba min-ni ahadun la-kana

guilty of acts of sinful disobedience, because they are the ones
min ahli'l-ma'asi li-anna-hum

endowed with a sense of inadequacy and a feeling of remorse.'"
ashabu'l-'ajzi wa'n-nadam.

"Then He said to me: 'O Supreme Helper,
thumma qala li ya Ghawthu'l-A'zamu'l-'ajzu

the sense of personal inadequacy is the source of radiant lights,
manba'u'l-anwari

while vain conceit is the source of gloomy darkness.'"
wa'l-'ujbu manba'u'z-zulma.

"Then He said to me: 'O Supreme Helper,
thumma qala li ya Ghawthu'l-A'zamu

those guilty of acts of sinful disobedience are veiled by their acts
ahlu'l-ma'asi mahjubuna bi'l-ma'asi

of sinful disobedience, while those performing acts of worshipful obedience
wa ahlu't-ta'ati

are veiled by their acts of worshipful obedience.
mahjubuna bi't-ta'at:

I have other folk behind them, folk who do not suffer the distress of acts
wa li wara'a-hum qawmun akharuna laisa la-hum

of sinful disobedience, nor the anxiety of acts of worshipful obedience.'"
ghammu'l-ma'asi wa la hammu't-ta'at.

"Then He said to me: 'O Supreme Helper,
thumma qala li ya Ghawthu'l-A'zamu

convey to the sinners the good news of grace and generous favour,
bashshiri'l-mudhnibina bi'l-fadli wa'l-karam:

and convey to the vainly conceited the grim tidings of justice and retribution.'"
wa bashshiri'l-mu'jibina bi'l-'adli wa'n-naqam.

"Then He said to me: 'O Supreme Helper,
thumma qala li ya Ghawthu'l-A'zamu

the people of worshipful obedience are mindful of the blessing,
ahlu't-ta'ati yadhkuruna'n-na'im:

while the people of sinful disobedience are mindful of the All-Compassionate.'"
wa ahlu'l-ma'asi yadhkuruna'r-Rahim.

"Then He said to me: 'O Supreme Helper,
thumma qala li ya Ghawthu'l-A'zamu

I am Near to the disobedient sinner after he desists
Ana Qaribun ila'l-'asi ba'da ma yafraghu

from sinful disobedience, but I am Distant from the obedient worshipper
mina'l-'isyan: wa Ana Ba'idun mina'l-muti'i

after he has finished performing acts of worshipful obedience.'"
ba'da ma faragha mina't-ta'at.

"Then He said to me: 'O Supreme Helper,
thumma qala li ya Ghawthu'l-A'zamu

I created the common folk, but they could not behold the light
khalaqtu'l-'awamma fa-lam yutiqu nura

of My splendour, for I set between Me and them the veil of darkness.
baha'i fa-ja'altu baini wa baina-hum hijaba'z-zulma:

I also created the privileged few, but they could not come close to Me,
wa khalaqtu'l-khawassa fa-lam yutiqu mujawarati

for I set the lights between Me and them, as a screen.'"
fa-ja'altu'l-anwara baini wa baina-hum hijaba.

"Then He said to me: 'O Supreme Helper,
thumma qala li ya Ghawthu'l-A'zamu

tell your companions [that I say]: "If anyone among you wishes
qul li-ashabi-ka man arada min-hum

to attain to Me, he must practice detachment
an yasila ilayya fa-'alai-hi bi'l-khuruji

from everything apart from Me.""
'an kulli shai'in siwa'i.

"Then He said to me: 'O Supreme Helper, depart
thumma qala li ya Ghawthu'l-A'zamu'khruj

from the last remnant of this world, and you will attain to the Hereafter.
'an'uqbati'd-dunya tasil bi'l-akhira:

Depart from the last remnant of the Hereafter, and you will attain to Me."
wa'khruj'an'uqbati'l-akhirati tasil ilayya.

"Then He said to me: 'O Supreme Helper, you must become detached
thumma qala li ya Ghawthu'l-A'zamu'khruj

from the physical forms and the natural instincts. Then become detached
'ani'l-ajsami wa'n-nufus: thumma'khruj

from the hearts and the spirits. Then become detached from the law
'ani'l-qulubi wa'l-arwah: thumma'khruj mina'l-hukmi

and the commandment, and you will attain to Me."
wa'l-amri tasil ilayya.

"I then said: 'O my Lord, which ritual prayer [salat]* is closest to You?"
fa-qultu ya Rabbi ayyu salatin aqrabu ilai-k.

"He replied: 'The ritual prayer in which there is nothing apart from Me,
qala's-salat allati laisa fi-ha siwaya

while the one performing the prayer is absent from it
wa sahibu-ha gha'ibun'an-ha

and invisible because of it."
wa gha'ibun bi-ha.

"Then I said: 'O my Lord, which fast is most meritorious in Your sight?"
thumma qultu ya Rabbi ayyu sawmin afdalu'inda-ka

"He replied: 'The fast in which there is nothing apart from Me,
qala's-sawmu'lladhi laisa fi-hi siwaya

while the one who is fasting is absent from it.'"
wa's-sa'imu gha'ibun'an-h.

"Then I said: 'Which deed is most meritorious in Your sight?'"
thumma qultu ayyu'amalin afdalu'inda-k.

"He replied: 'The deed in which there is nothing apart from Me,
qala'l-'amal alladhi laisa fi-hi siwaya

no trace of the Garden [of Paradise] and the Fire [of Hell],
min al-janna wa'n-nar

while the one who is doing it is absent from it.'"
wa sahibu-hu gha'ib'an-hu

"Then I said: 'O my Lord, which kind of weeping
thumma qultu ya Rabbi ayyu buka'in

is most meritorious in Your sight?"
afdalu'inda-k.

"He replied: 'The weeping of those who laugh.'"
qala buka'u'd-dahikin.

"Then I said: 'O my Lord, which kind of laughter
thumma qultu ya Rabbi ayyu dahkin

is most meritorious in Your sight?'"
afdalu'inda-k.

"He replied: 'The laughter of the penitent weepers.'"
qala dahku'l-bakina't-ta'ibin.

"Then I said: 'O my Lord, which kind of repentance
thumma qultu ya Rabbi ayyu tawbatin

is most meritorious in Your sight?"
afdalu'inda-k.

"He replied: 'The repentance of the virtuous.'"
qala tawbatu'l-ma'sumin.

"Then I said: 'O my Lord, which kind of virtuousness
thumma qultu ya Rabbi ayyu'ismatin

is most meritorious in Your sight?'"
afdalu'inda-k.

"He replied: 'The virtuousness of those who repent.'"
qala'ismatu't-ta'ibin.

"He also said to me: 'O Supreme Helper, the seeker of knowledge
wa qala li ya Ghawthu'l-A'zamu laisa li-talibi'l-'ilmi

has no way forward in My sight, except after his admission of ignorance,
'indi sabilun illa ba'da inkari-hi

because, if he did not abandon the knowledge in his possession,
li-anna-hu law lam yatruki'l-'ilma'lladhi'inda-hu

he would become a devil.'"
sara shaitana.

The Supreme Helper went on to say: "I saw the Lord (Exalted is He),
qala'l-Ghawthu'l-A'zamu ra'aitu'r-Rabba (ta'ala)

so I asked Him: "O my Lord, what is the meaning of ardent love?"
fa-sa'altu-hu ya Rabbi ma ma'na'l-'ishq.

"He said to me: 'O Supreme Helper, [it means that] you must love Me
wa qala li ya Ghawthu'l-A'zamu''shaq li

ardently, and empty your heart of everything apart from Me.'"
wa afrigh qalba-ka'an siwaya.

"He also said to me: 'O Supreme Helper,
wa qala li ya Ghawthu'l-A'zamu

once you have experienced the outward form of ardent love,
idha'arafta zahira'l-'ishqi

you must become extinct to ardent love, because it is a veil
fa-'alai-ka bi'l-fana'i'ani'l-'ishqi li-anna-hu

between the ardent lover and the ardently Beloved.'"
hijabun baina'l-'ashiq wa'l-ma'shuq.

"He also said to me: 'O Supreme Helper,
wa qala li ya Ghawthu'l-A'zamu

when you intend to make repentance, in is incumbent upon you
idha aradta't-tawbata fa-'alai-ka

to evict the trouble of sin from the lower self, then to rid the heart
'ani'n-nafsi thumma bi-ikhraji khatarati-hi'ani'l-qalbi

of its thoughts and emotions, so that you may attain to Me.
bi-ikhraji hammi'dh-dhanbi tasil ilayya

You must also be patient, for if you do not practice patience,
fa-'sbir fa-in lam tasbir

you will be included among the scornful.'"
fa-anta min al-mustahzi'in

"He also said to me: 'O Supreme Helper, when you intend
wa qala li ya Ghawthu'l-A'zamu idha aradta

to enter the Sanctuary, you must not pay any attention to the Kingdom,
an tadkhula ila harami fa-la taltafit ila'l-mulki

nor to the Sovereignty, nor to the Dominion, because the Kingdom
wa'l-malakuti wa la ila'l-jabaruti li-anna al-mulka

is the devil of the scholar, while the Sovereignty is the devil of him
shaitanu'l-'alimi wa'l-malakutu shaitanu'l-'arifi

who learns by direct experience, and the Dominion is the devil of him
wa'l-jabarutu shaitanu'l-waqifi

who is fully aware. If someone is satisfied with any one of them, he is included among the outcasts in My sight."
fa-man radiya bi-wahidin min-ha fa-huwa'indi min al-matrudin.

"He also said to me: 'O Supreme Helper, the spiritual struggle is one
wa qala li ya Ghawthu'l-A'zamu'l-mujahadatu bahrun

of the oceans of direct vision, and it is preferred by those who are fully aware.

min bihari al-mushahadati wa'khtara-hu'l-waqifun:

If someone intends to enter the ocean of direct vision,
fa-man arada'd-dukhula fi bahri'l-mushahadati

it is therefore incumbent upon him to choose the spiritual struggle,
fa-'alai-hi bi'khtiyari al-mujahadata

because that struggle is the seed of direct vision.
li-anna'l-mujahadata badhr al-mushahadati

Direct vision without the spiritual struggle is inconceivable.
wa'l-mushahadatu bi-duna'l-mujahadati muhal:

If someone chooses the spiritual struggle,
man ikhtara'l-mujahadata

he will have the direct vision of Me, whether he wishes or not."
fa-la-hu mushahadati in sha' aw aba

"He also said to me: 'O Supreme Helper,
wa qala li ya Ghawthu'l-A'zamu

the seekers cannot do without the spiritual struggle,
la budda li't-talibina min al-mujahada:

just as they cannot do without Me.'"
ka-ma la budda la-hum min-ni.

"He also said to me: 'O Supreme Helper,
wa qala li ya Ghawthu'l-A'zamu

the dearest of servants to Me is a servant who has a father and a son,
inna ahabba'l-'ibadi ilayya'abdun kana la-hu'l-walidu wa'l-waladu

yet his heart is empty of them. If his father were to die, he would not
wa qalbu-hu farighun min-huma law mata la-hu'l-walidu

suffer grief because of his father's death, and if his son were to die,
laisa la-hu huznun bi-mawt walidi-hi wa law mata la-hu'l-waladu

he would not suffer distress because of his son's death.
laisa la-hu hammun bi-mawt al-waladi

Once the servant has reached this degree and this station,
fa-idha balagha'l-'abdu hadhihi'l-martabata wa'l-manzilata

he is in My presence with neither father nor son,
fa-huwa'indi bi-la walidin wa la waladin

and there is none comparable unto him.'"
wa lam yakun la-hu kufuwan ahad.

"He also said to me: 'O Supreme Helper,
wa qala li ya Ghawthu'l-A'zamu

if someone does not taste the extinction of the father in My affection,
man lam yadhuq fana'a'l-walidi bi-mahabbati

and the extinction of the son in My love,
wa fana'a'l-waladi bi-mawaddati

he will not discover the delight of Unique Singularity.'"
lam yajid ladhdhata'l-Wahdaniyyati'l-Fardaniyya.

"He also said to me: 'O Supreme Helper,
wa qala li ya Ghawthu'l-A'zamu

if you intend to look toward Me in every situation,
idha aradta an tanzura ilayya fi kulli mahallin

you must choose a sad heart that is empty of everything apart from Me.'"
fa'khtar qalban hazinan khaliyan'am-ma siwaya.

"Then I said: 'O my Lord, what is the knowledge of knowledge?'
thumma qultu ya Rabbi ma'ilmu'l-'ilm.

"He replied: 'The knowledge of knowledge is the ignorance of knowledge.'"
qala'ilmu'l-'ilmi huwa'l-jahlu'ani'l-'ilm.

"He also said to me: 'O Supreme Helper, congratulations
wa qala li ya Ghawthu'l-A'zamu

are due to a servant whose heart inclines to the spiritual struggle,
tuba li-'abdin mala qalbu-hu ila'l-mujahadati

but woe unto a servant whose heart inclines to the desires of the flesh!'"
wa wailun li-'abdin mala qalbu-hu ila'sh-shahawat.

"Then I asked the Lord (Exalted is He) about the Heavenly Ascension.
thumma sa'altu'r-Rabbi (ta'ala)'ani'l-Mi'raj.

"He said: 'It is the ascension beyond everything apart from Me,
qala huwa'l-'uruju'an kulli shai'in siwa'i

and the perfection of the Heavenly Ascension is:
wa kamalu'l-Mi'raji

The eye did not turn aside, nor was it overbold.'"
ma zagha'l-basaru wa ma tagha. (53:17)

"Then He said to me: 'O Supreme Helper, there is no ritual prayer
thumma qala li ya Ghawthu'l-A'zamu la salata

for one who has no Heavenly Ascension in My sight.'"
li-man la Mi'raja la-hu'indi.

"Then He said to me: 'O Supreme Helper, he who is deprived
thumma qala li ya Ghawthu'l-A'zamu'l-mahrumu

of the ritual prayer, he is the one who is deprived
'ani's-salati huwa'l-mahrumu

of the Heavenly Ascension in My sight.'"
'ani'l-Mi'raji'indi.

*****

This brings us to the conclusion of al-Ghawthiyya, which is also called al-Mi'rajiyya, through the enabling grace of Allah (Exalted is He and Mighty is His Authority).

WIRD DA'WAT AL-JALALA
LITANY OF THE INVOCATION OF SUBLIME MAJESTY
by Shaikh 'Abd al-Qadir (sanctified be his innermost being).

· *In the Name of Allah, the All-Merciful, the All-Compassionate.*
Bismi'llahi'r-Rahmani'r-Rahim.

Note: After the recitation, you should pronounce the following solemn vow of dedication:

For the presence of the Supreme Helper and the venerated Cardinal Pole,
li-hadrati'l-Ghawthi'l-A'Dami wa'l-Qutbi'l-mu'addami'sh-Shaikhi

Shaikh Muhyi'd-Din'Abd al-Qadir al-Gilani.
Muhyi'd-Dini'Abdi'l-Qadiri'l-Gilani.

May Allah sanctify his innermost being,
qaddasa'llahu sirra-hu

and may He illuminate his mausoleum,
wa nawwira dariha-hu

and may He be well pleased with him.
wa radiya'an-hu

May He grant us the blessed benefits of his many forms of knowledge,
wa nafa'-na bi-barakati'ulumi-hi

and may He support us with his noble means of support,
wa amadda-na bi-imdadati-hi'sh-sharifati

together with all the loving and beloved seekers.
ma'a jami'i'l-muridina'l-muhibbina'l-mahbubin.

Amin.

The litany reads as follows:

In the Name of Allah, the All-Merciful, the All-Compassionate.
Bismi'llahi'r-Rahmani'r-Rahim.

O Allah, I beseech You by the upright letter Alif,
Allahumma inni as'alu-ka bi'l-Alifi'l-qa'imi'lladhi

which has none preceding it,
laisa qabla-hu sabiqun

and by the two Lams, with which You have erased the secrets,
wa bi'l-Lamaini'llataini tamasta bi-hima'l-asrara

and the pair of which you have placed between the mind and the spirit,
wa ja'alta-huma baina'l-'aqli wa'r-ruhi

and have imposed upon them the sure covenant.
wa akhadhta'alai-hima'l-'ahda'l-wathiq.

[I also beseech You] by the letter Ha', which encompasses
wa bi'l-Ha'i'l-muhitati

the sciences of inanimate and moving objects,
bi'l-'ulumi'l-jawamidi wa'l-mutaharrikati

and of speechless beings and those endowed with speech.
wa's-sawamiti wa'n-nawatiq.

I also implore You, O Allah, by Your Supremely Splendid Name, which is:
wa as'alu-ka Allahumma bi'smi-ka'l-'aDimi'l-a'Dam:

He is Allah; there is no god but He.
Huwa'llahu'lladhi la ilaha illa Hu:

[He is] the All-Merciful, the All-Compassionate,
ar-Rahmanu'r-Rahim.

{He is] the King, the Holy One, [the Source of] Peace,
al-Maliku'l-Quddusu's-Salamu'l-

the Safe-keeper, the Guardian, the All-Splendid,
Mu'minu'l-Muhaiminu'l-'Azizu'l-

the All-Compelling, the All-Sublime.
Jabbaru'l-Mutakabbir. (59:22,23)

[He is] the Light, the Guide, the Originator, the All-Powerful,
an-Nuru'l-Hadi'l-Badi'u'l-Qadiru'l-

the All-Compelling, the One who radiated and so transcended,
Qahiru'lladhi tasha'sha'a fa-'rtafa'a

and subjugated and so prevailed, and cast a glance at the mountain,
wa qahara fa-sada'a wa naDara naDratan li'l-jabali

so that it split asunder and Moses fell stunned by the shock.
fa-taqatta'a wa kharra Musa sa'iqan mina'l-faza'.

You are Allah, the God Most Generous, Eternal and Everlasting,
Anta'llahu'l-Ilahu'l-Akramu'l-Azaliyyu's-Sarmadiyyu'lladhi

the One who never changes, and by whom our minds are perplexed.
la yahulu tad'hashu min-hu'l-'uqul.

O Allah, I beseech You, by the secret of the secret,
Allahumma inni as'alu-ka bi-sirri sirri'lladhi

which You have promised to the hearts of the people of remembrance,
huwa Anta wa'adta bi-hi quluba ahli'dh-dhikri

in the hidden circuit of Your intimate knowledge,
bi-khafiyyi jawalani ma'rifati-ka

immerse me through contemplation, O Allah, O Allah, O Allah,
bi'l-fikri'ghmis-ni ya Allahu ya Allahu ya Allahu

in the ocean of Your lights, and fill my heart
fi bahri anwari-ka wa'mla' qalbi

with Your secrets, and establish me in You and because of You.
min asrari-ka wa makkin-ni fi-ka wa min-k.

I implore You to grant access to the secret
wa as'alu-ka'l-wusula bi's-sirri'lladhi

by which our minds are perplexed, for one is baffled by its nearness.
tad'hashu min-hu'l-'uqulu fa-huwa min qurbi-hi dhahil.

Atinukh Ba', Amlukh Ba'-Alif-Ya', Atinukhin Ba' Amlukhin Ba'-Alif-Ya'
and Amn Alif-Ya' and Amn Mihyash
wa Amnin Alif-Ya' wa Amnin Mihyashini'lladhi

—of the One who owns the sovereignty of the heavens and the earth.
la-hu mulku's-samawati wa'l-ard.

O Allah, my hearing and my sight,

Allahumma inna sam'i wa basari

my private and my public self, my inner and my outer being,
wa sirri wa jahri wa batini wa Dahiri

all bear witness to Your Singularity,
yashhadu la-ka bi'l-Wahdaniyyati'j'al-ni

so grant me direct vision of the Radiant Power.
ushahidu'l-Qudrata'n-Nuraniyya:

O Allah, He!
ya Allahu Hu.

At this point, you should appeal for whatever you wish to receive, [before going on to recite]:

O He to Whom the appeal for help is made,
ya Man yustaghathu bi-hi

when there is no ordinary helper to be found,
idha'udima'l-mughithu

and to Whom the appeal for support is made,
wa yustansaru bi-hi

when there is no ordinary supporter to be found,
idha'udima'n-nasiru

and of Whom we avail ourselves,
wa yunfa'u bi-hi

when the doors of the dumbfounded kings are locked,
idha ghulliqat abwabu'l-muluki'l-murtajati

and the heedless hearts conceal Him.
wa hajabat-hu'l-qulubu'l-ghafila.

It is pointless to hope for anything, except from You.
Tahfalushini'nqata'a'r-raja'u illa min-ka

The roads are all blocked, except those that lead to You.
wa suddati't-turuqu illa ilai-ka

All expectations are disappointed, except those that depend on You.
wa khabati'l-amalu illa fi-k.

O Helper, make haste! O Helper, make haste!
wa-Ghawth-ahu'l-'ajal: wa-Ghawth-ahu'l-'ajal.

[I am lost] if You do not answer my plea!
illa ajabta da'wati

And satisfy my need, and remove the veil from my sight!
wa'qdi hajati wa'kshif'an basirati.

—Three times.

There is no power nor any strength
wa la hawla wa la quwwata

except with Allah, the All-High, the Almighty.
illa bi'llahi'l-'Aliyyi'l-'ADim.

May Allah bless our master Muhammad and his family
wa salla'llahu'ala sayyidi-na Muhammadin wa'ala ali-hi

and his Companions, and may He grant them peace
wa ashabi-hi wa sallama tasliman

until the Day of Reckoning.
ila Yawmi'd-Din.

And praise be to Allah, the Lord of All the Worlds.
wa'l-hamdu li'llahi Rabbi'l-'alamin.

*****

WIRD AS-SUBH
THE LITANY OF THE DAYBREAK [WIRD AS-SUBH]

The marvellous exploits [manaqib] of our master, the Cardinal Pole of Cardinal Poles [Qutb al-aqtab], 'Abd al-Qadir al-Jilani.

He is Abu Salih, my master, 'Abd al-Qadir ibn Musa ibn 'Abdi'llah ibn Yahya az-Zahid ibn Muhammad ibn Dawud ibn Musa al-Jawn ibn 'Abdi'llah al-Haddi ibn al-Hasan ibn al-Muthanna ibn 'Ali ibn Abi Talib (may Allah the Exalted be well pleased with them all).

He was born (may Allah the Exalted be well pleased with him) in the year [A.H.] 470, and he died in [A.H.] 561. He was buried (may Allah be well pleased with him) in Baghdad.

People have singled him out as the subject of literary composition, and we shall mention, if Allah (Exalted is He) so wills, a small selection from his marvellous exploits [manaqib], containing instruction and benefit for the listener.

Let us therefore acknowledge that we depend for success on Allah's enabling grace [tawfiq], and let me introduce myself as the pauper in need of the mercy of Allah the Almighty, Habib Muhammad, son of the learned Shaikh Sidq Muhammad Ibrahim, al-Qahiri [the Cairene] by place of birth, al-Qadiri al-Ash'ari by spiritual disposition [mashrab] and theological doctrine [mu'taqad].

In the work entitled Bahjat al-Asrar [The Splendour of the Mysteries], the author cites a reliable chain of transmission [isnad], by which the following report is traced to that exemplary guide, Shaikh Shihab ad-Din Abu'l-Hafs Muhammad ibn Muhammad ibn 'Abdi'llah as-Suhrawardi, who said:

"I once heard Shaikh Muhyi'd-Din 'Abd al-Qadir say, speaking from the lectern in his schoolhouse: 'Every saint [wali] is on the footprint of a Prophet [Nabi], and I am on the footprint of my ancestor, Muhammad (Allah bless him and give him peace). Whenever the Chosen One [al-Mustafa] (Allah bless him and give him peace) raises a foot, I place my feet in the spot from which he has raised his foot-unless it is one of the footprints of Prophethood [Nubuwwa], in which case there can be no means of access to it for anyone other than a Prophet.'"

In the same work, Shaikh Abu'Amr'Uthman ibn Marzuq is reported as having said:

"No one participated with him-that is to say, with Shaikh 'Abd al-Qadir al-Gilani (may Allah be well pleased with him)-in his spiritual states, his station and his secrets, apart from the Prophets (blessing and peace be upon them). Nor was anyone endowed with superior grace in this spiritual path, apart from Allah (Almighty and Glorious is He) and His Messenger Muhammad (Allah bless him and give him peace)."

In the work entitled Lata'if al-Minan [Subtleties of Gracious Favours], by Ibn 'Ata'u'llah as-Sikandari ash-Shadhili, it is reported that Abu's-Sa'ud ibn ash-Shibli (may Allah be well pleased with him) once said, referring to the Greatest Shaikh [Ibn al-'Arabi]:

"I am in the service of the Shaikh who did not leave his special grace to anyone else...."

In the work entitled Qala'id al-Jawahir [Necklaces of Gems], we are told:

"It must be understood that gracious favour is in the Hand of Allah, and that He bestows it upon whomever He will, for Allah is the Owner of Splendid Grace [wa'llahu Dhu'l-fadli'l-'azim]. Nevertheless, it is true to say that in none of the Shaikhs and masters of spiritual states, after the Companions (may Allah be well pleased with them), has there been such a combination of charismatic exploits [manaqib] and praiseworthy qualities, as those combined in our master and our Shaikh, Shaikh 'Abd al-Qadir al-Jilani (may Allah be well pleased with him), in respect of practice and knowledge ['amal wa'ilm], noble descent and lineage [hasab wa nasab], talents and blessings...."

In the work entitled Zain al-Majalis [Beauty of the Sessions], we read:

"Suppose it should be asked: 'How do you account for the response of Shaikh 'Abd al-Wahhab ash-Sha'rani to the saying of Shaikh 'Abd al-Qadir al-Jilani (may Allah be well pleased with him): 'This foot of mine is upon the neck of every saint of Allah'? Why did he restrict its application to the people of his own generation?' The answer to this must be: 'When the Shaikh restricted its application, he was considering the greatest of the saints [awliya'], those who were superior even to him [Shaikh 'Abd al-Qadir], meaning the Companions (may Allah be well pleased with them), not those of lower rank in any generation whatsoever, even if they were also saints. Compare the reservation of Shaikh al-Imam Jalal ad-Din al-Muhalla, in connection with the story of Moses (peace be upon him) and concerning the words of Allah (Exalted is He):

O Moses! I have preferred you above [all] the people.
ya Musa inni'stafaitu-ka'ala'n-nasi. (7:144)

"This he interpreted as referring only to the people of his [Moses'] own time, in consideration of those [later] Prophets (blessing and peace be upon them) who would be superior to Moses."

In the work entitled Bahjat al-Asrar [The Splendour of the Mysteries], toward the end of the report attributed to Shaikh Abu'l-Qasim ibn Bakr Ahmad, it is stated that:

"The Lord of Truth (Exalted is He) said to him [Shaikh 'Abd al-Qadir], in the language of the Unseen: 'Today you are in Our presence, established, secure', and He seated him in the company of the spirits of the Prophets [arwah an-Nabiyyin], on a platform between this world and the Hereafter, between the creation and the Creator, between the outer [zahir] and the inner [batin], between what is within reach and that which is out of reach. He also gave him four faces: (1) a face with which he can look toward this lower world, (2) a face with which he can look toward the Hereafter, (3) a face with which he can look toward the creation [khalq], and (4) a face with which he can look toward the Creator [Khaliq]...."

In his book entitled Khulasat al-Mafakhir [Synopsis of Glorious Deeds and Qualities], Shaikh 'Abdu'llah al-Yafi'i has declared:

"Shaikh 'Abd al-Qadir al-Jilani (may Allah be well pleased with him) is the highest in spiritual station, after the Companions, of all the saints [awliya']."

According to the experts in Reality [muhaqqiqun], the spiritual station of Shaikh 'Abd al-Qadir al-Jilani is "the highest of all the fundamental sources [usul]."

By advancing irrefutable evidence, the compiler of Zain al-Majalis [Beauty of the Sessions] has refuted the statement of the Greatest Shaikh [ash-Shaikh al-Akbar], concerning the superior elevation of the station of Ibn ash-Shibli (may Allah be well pleased with him) above the station of Shaikh 'Abd al-Qadir al-Jilani. It is possible, of course, that the statement attributed to the Greatest Shaikh [ash-Shaikh al-Akbar], concerning the superior elevation of the station of Ibn ash-Shibli, was falsely ascribed to him, because he [Ibn ash-Shibli] once said: "I am in the service of the Shaikh who did not leave his special grace to anyone else." Allah knows best.

It was the Cardinal Pole and Renewer [of the Faith] [al-Qutb al-Mujaddid], the highly erudite Shaikh Sadaqatu'llah, the son of the saint [wali] Shaikh Sulaiman al-Qahiri, who said:

All of the parties are agreed in unanimity, of one accord concerning your perfection in your exaltation.
kullu't-tawa'ifi bi'l-ijma'i muttafiqah 'ala kamali-ka fi'ulya-ka muttasiqah

Even the Kharijites, the people of deviation, and the atheists [agree that] you are the pivotal point for every Reviver of the Faith.

hatta'l-Khawariji ahli'z-zaighi wa'z-Zandaqah anta'l-madaru li-kulli Muhyi'd-Din.

All of this leads us, on the basis of the decisive proofs that have been cited, and the unambiguous reports that are so well known, to the conclusion that there can be none higher, none superior, and none more noble in spiritual station, in deeds, and in quality of innermost being, among the earlier and the later saints [awliya'], until the Day of Resurrection [Yawm al-Qiyama], than our master 'Abd al-Qadir al-Jilani (may Allah be well pleased with him). So said 'Abd al-Karim al-Jili (may Allah be well pleased with him).

This is the moment for us to embark on an account of the litanies [awrad] recited by the Helper [Ghawth] (may Allah sanctify his splendid innermost being) at the five times of day, as well as the litanies [awrad] of the week, the greatest invocation of blessing [as-salat al-kubra] and other benedictions [salawat], the plea for victory [du'a 'an-nasr], the recital of sublimity [hizb al-jalala] and the supplication of the litany of sublimity [wird al-jalala], and other observances [waza'if]. The first of these is the Litany of the Daybreak [Wird as-Sabah], which is also called the Recital of Humble Entreaty [Hizb al-Ibtihal]. Its historical background is as follows:

In the Name of Allah, the All-Merciful, the All-Compassionate
Bismi'llahi'r-Rahmani'r-Rahim

This noble and blessed litany [wird] is the composition of the lordly scholar, the radiant candle, the master of indication and meanings, the Shaikh of Islam, the Reviver of the Religion and the Faith [Muhyi'l-Milla wa'd-Din], Shaikh Abu Salih 'Abd al-Qadir al-Gilani. May Allah sanctify his innermost being, and may He bestow his goodness and his righteousness upon us, and upon all the seekers and lovers [of the Truth].

It has been transmitted by Shaikh al-Islam Kamal ad-Din ibn Abi Sharif, on the authority of the Cardinal Pole of the Age [Qutb az-Zaman], Abu'l-'Awn al-Ghuzzi (may Allah bestow His mercy upon him), from Shaikh al-Islam Shihab ad-Din Raslan ar-Ramli (sanctified be his innermost being), from the lordly scholar Nasru'llah al-Jadali (sanctified be his innermost being), from 'Abdu'llah ibn an-Nasih (may Allah bestow His mercy upon him), from 'Abdu'llah ibn Muhammad al-'Ajami (may Allah bestow His mercy upon him). The latter was blessed with long life, for the year of his birth was [A.H.] 546, and the year of his death was [A.H.] 731, which means that he died at the age of one hundred and eighty-five. He said:

"He informed me of it [the litany], and with it he invested me with the skullcap ['arraqiyya] of the Cardinal Pole of the Age [Qutb az-Zaman]-the one to whom the necks of the saints [awliya'] were humbly bowed, in the West and in the East, Arabs and non-Arabs alike-the Sultan of the saints, Muhyi'd-Din Abu Muhammad as-Sayyid ash-Shaikh 'Abd al-Qadir al-Gilani (sanctified be his innermost being), the son of Abu Salih Musa Jangidost. May Allah (Exalted is He) enable us to derive benefit from him, and may He install us within his blessed grace."

This is the litany [wird] to which he referred. It is sometimes called the Litany of the Daybreak [Wird as-Subh], and it is also called the Incantation of Humble Entreaty [Hizb al-Ibtihal]. The proper time for its recitation is after the obligatory ritual prayer of daybreak [faridat as-subh], once every day. We have absolute permission to perform it, from our present Shaikhs, and from the paternal uncle of my grandfather, my own Shaikh now deceased, Sayyid Shaikh Mahmud Efendi, offspring of the late Sayyid al-Hajj Zakariyya Efendi al-Gilani al-Baghdadi, the President [Naqib] of the chieftains in Baghdad (may Allah sanctify his innermost being), and from my paternal cousin and my Shaikh, Sayyid Muhammad Mukarram Efendi, offspring of the late Sayyid Shaikh Muhammad Efendi al-Gilani al-Azhari al-Hamawi (may Allah sanctify his innermost being), whose residence is in Hamah (may Allah keep him [hamma-hu] in His protection [Hima-h]).

This really is the moment to embark on the blessed litany [wird] :

WIRD AS-SUBH - 1
THE LITANY OF THE DAYBREAK [WIRD AS-SUBH], ALSO CALLED THE RECITAL OF HUMBLE ENTREATY [HIZB AL-IBTIHAL].

In the Name of Allah, the All-Merciful, the All-Compassionate
Bismi'llahi'r-Rahmani'r-Rahim

Praise be to Allah, Lord of All the Worlds,
al-hamdu li'llahi Rabbi'l-'alamin:

the All-Merciful, the All-Compassionate,
ar-Rahmani'r-Rahi:.

Master of the Day of Reckoning.
Maliki yawmi'd-din:

You alone do we worship, and of You alone do we seek help.
iyya-ka na'budu wa iyya-ka nasta'in:

Guide us in the straight path,
ihdina's-sirata'l-mustaqim:

the path of those whom You have blessed,
sirata'lladhina an'amta'alai-him:

not of those who earn Your wrath,
ghairi'l-maghdubi'alai-him wa la'd-dallin. (1:1-7)

In the Name of Allah, the All-Merciful, the All-Compassionate
Bismi'llahi'r-Rahmani'r-Rahim

Alif, Lam, Mim.
Alif-Lam-Mim :

This is the Book, no doubt about it; a guidance for the righteous,
dhalika'l-Kitabu la raiba fi-h: hudan li'l-muttaqin:

who believe in the Unseen, and perform the prayer,
alladhina yu'minuna bi'l-ghaibi wa yuqimuna's-salata

and spend out of what We have provided for them;
wa mimma razaqna-hum yunfiqun :

who believe in what has been sent down to you,
wa'lladhina yu'minuna bi-ma unzila ilai-ka

and what has been sent down before you,
wa ma unzila min qabli-k :

and are certain of the Hereafter.
wa bi'l-akhirati hum yuqinun :

These follow guidance from their Lord,
ula'ika'ala hudan min Rabbi-him

and it is they who will prosper.
wa ula'ika humu'l-muflihun. (2:1-5)

Your God is One God.
wa Ilahu-kum Ilahun Wahid :

There is no god but He, the All Merciful, the All-Compassionate.
la ilaha illa Huwa'r-Rahmanu'r-Rahim. (2:163)

Allah! There is no god but He, the Living, the Eternal.
Allahu la ilaha illa Huwa'l-Hayyu'l-Qayyum.

Neither slumber nor sleep can overtake Him.

la ta'khudhu-hu sinatun wa la nawm.

To Him belongs whatever there is in the heavens
la-hu ma fi's-samawati

and whatever there is in the earth.
wa ma fi'l-ard.

Who is there to intercede with Him save by His leave?
man dha'lladhi yashfa'u'inda-hu illa bi-idhni-h.

He knows what is in front of them and what is behind them,
ya'lamu ma baina aidi-him wa ma khalfa-hum

while they encompass nothing of His knowledge save what He will.
wa la yuhituna bi-shai'in min'ilmi-hi illa bi-ma sha'.

His throne comprises the heavens and the earth,
wasi'a kursiyyu-hu's-samawati wa'l-ard :

and He is never weary of preserving them.
wa la ya'udu-hu hifzu-huma :

He is the All-High, the All-Glorious.
wa Huwa'l-'Aliyyu'l-'Azim. (2:255)

There is no compulsion in religion.
la ikraha fi'd-din:

The right direction is henceforth distinct from error.
qad tabayyana'r-rushdu mina'l-ghayy :

And he who rejects false deities, and believes in Allah,
fa-man yakfur bi't-taghuti wa yu'min bi'llahi

has grasped the most secure handle, which will never break.
fa-qadi'stamsaka bi'l-'urwati'l-wuthqa la'nfisama la-ha.

Allah is All-Hearing, All-Knowing.
wa'llahu Sami'un'Alim. (2:256)

Allah is the Protecting Friend of those who believe.
Allahu Waliyyu'lladhina amanu

He brings them out of the darkness into the light.
yukhriju-hum mina'z-zulumati ila'n-nur.

As for those who disbelieve, their patrons are the false deities.
wa'lladhina kafaru awliya'u-humu't-Taghutu

They bring them out of light into darkness.
yukhrijuna-hum mina'n-nuri

Such are the rightful owners of the Fire,
ila'z-zulumat : ula'ika

wherein they shall dwell eternally.
ashabu'n-nari hum fi-ha khalidun. (2:257)

Allah bears witness that there is no god but He-
shahida'llahu anna-hu la ilaha illa Huwa

and [so do] the angels and the men of learning-upholding justice.
wa'l-mala'ikatu wa ulu'l-'ilmi qa'iman bi'l-qist :

There is no god but He, the Omnipotent, the All-Wise.
qa'iman bi'l-qist : la ilaha

the Omnipotent, the All-Wise.
la ilaha illa Huwa'l-'Azizu'l-Hakim. (3:18)

The true religion in the sight of Allah is surrender [to His will and guidance].
inna' d-dina'inda'llahi'l-islam

Those who received the Book differed only after
wa ma'khtalafa'lladhina utu'l-Kitaba

knowledge came to them, through transgression among themselves.
illa min ba'di ma ja'a-humu'l-'ilmu baghyan baina-hum :

Whoever disbelieves the signs of Allah, Allah is Swift at reckoning.
wa man yakfur bi-ayati'llahi fa-inna'llaha Sari'u'l-hisab. (3:19)

And if they argue with you, say: "I have surrendered
fa-in hajju-ka fa-qul aslamtu

my purpose to Allah and so have those who follow me."
aslamtu wajhiya li'llahi wa mani'ttaba'a-n :

And say to those who have received the Book
wa qul li'lladhina utu'l-Kitaba

and do not read: 'Have you surrendered?'
wa'l-ummiyyina a-aslamtum :

If they surrender, then they are rightly guided,
fa-in aslamu fa-qadi'htadaw :

and if they turn away, then it is your duty only to convey the message.
wa in tawallaw fa-inna-ma'alai-ka'l-balagh :

Allah is All-Seeing of His servants.
wa'llahu Basirun bi'l-'ibad. (3:20)

Lord is Allah who created the heavens and the earth
inna Rabba-ka'lladhi khalaqa's-samawati wa'l-arda

in six Days, then He mounted on the Throne.
fi sittati ayyamin thumma'stawa'ala'l-'Arsh :

He covers the night with the day, which is in haste to follow it,
yughshi'l-laila'n-nahara yatlubu-hu hathithan

and has made the sun and the moon
yatlubu-hu hathithan wa'sh-shamsa wa'l-qamara

and the stars subservient by His command.
wa'n-nujuma musakhkharatin bi-amri-h :

His is all creation and commandment.
a-la la-hu'l-khalqu wa'l-amr :

Blessed be Allah, the Lord of the Worlds!
tabaraka'llahu Rabbu'l-'alamin. (7:54)

Call upon your Lord humbly and in secret;
ud'u Rabba-kum tadarru'an wa khufya :

He does not love those who go too far in the wrong direction.
inna-hu la yuhibbu'l-mu'tadin. (7:55)

Do not cause confusion in the earth after the fair ordering thereof,
wa la tufsidu fi'l-ardi ba'da islahi-ha

and call on Him in fear and hope.
wa'd'u-hu khawfan wa tama'a :

The mercy of Allah is close indeed to those who do good.
inna rahmata'llahi qaribun mina'l-muhsinin. (7:56)

Say: "Cry to Allah, or cry to the All-Merciful.
quli'd'u'llaha awi'd'u'r-Rahman :

To whichever to cry, His are the Most Beautiful Names.
ayya-ma tad'u fa-la-hu'l-Asma'u'l-Husna :

And do not be loud voiced in your worship,
wa la tajhar bi's-salati-ka

nor yet silent therein; but follow a way between."
wa la tukhafit bi-ha wa'btaghi baina dhalika sabila. (17:110)

And say: "Praise be to Allah, who has not taken to Himself a son,
wa quli'l-hamdu li'llahi'lladhi lam yattakhidh waladan

and who has no partner in the Sovereignty,
wa lam yakun la-hu sharikun fi'l-mulki

nor has He any protecting friend through dependence.
wa lam yakun la-hu waliyyun mina'dh-dhulli

And magnify Him with magnificence."
wa kabbir-hu takbira. (17:111)

Allah is Supremely Great, by far!
Allahu Akbaru kabira

Praise be to Allah, with much and frequent praise!
wa'l-hamdu li'llahi hamdan kathira

Glory be to Allah, and His be the praise
wa subhana'llahi wa bi-hamdi-hi

in both the early morning and the evening time!
wa bi-hamdi-hi bukratan wa asila.

In the Name of Allah, the All-Merciful, the All-Compassionate
Bismi'llahi'r-Rahmani'r-Rahim

By those who set the ranks in battle order,
wa's-saffati saffan

and those who drive away with reproof,
fa-'z-zajirati zajran

and those who recite as a Reminder,
fa-'taliyati dhikran

your Lord is surely One;
inna Ilaha-kum la-Wahid :

Lord of the heavens and of the earth
Rabbu's-smaawati wa'l-ardi

and what is between them,
wa ma baina-huma

and Lord of the sun's risings.
wa Rabbu'l-mashariq.

We have adorned the lowest heaven
inna zayyanna's-sama'a'd-dunya

with the adornment of the planets,
bi-zinatini'l-kawakib :

with security from every rebellious devil.
wa hifzan min kulli shaitanin marid :

They cannot listen to the Highest Chiefs
la yassamma'unna

for they are pelted from every side,
ila'l-Mala'i'l-a'la wa yuqdhafuna min kulli janib.

outcast, and theirs is a perpetual torment;
duhuran wa la-hum'adhabun wasib.

Except him who snatches a fragment,
illa man khatifa'l-khatfata

and a piercing flame pursues him.
fa-atba'a-hu shihabun thaqib.

Then ask them: "Are they stronger as a creation,
fa-'stafti-him a-hum ashaddu khalqan

or those whom We have created?
am-man khalaqna :

We created them of plastic caly.
inna khalaqna-hum min tinin lazib. (37:1-11)

O company of jinn and men, if you have power to penetrate
ya ma'shara'l-jinni wa'l-insi ini'stata'tuman tanfudhu

the regions of the heavens and the earth, then penetrate!
min aqtari's-samawati wa'l-ardi fa-'nfudhu

You will never penetrate them except with sanction.
la tanfudhuna illa bi-sultan.

So which of the favours of your Lord do the two of you deny?
fa-bi-ayyi ala'i Rabbi-kuma tukadhdhiban.

There will be sent, against you both, heat of fire
yursalu'alai-kuma shuwazun min narin

and flash of brass, and you will not escape.
wa nuhasun fa-la tantasiran :

So which of the favours of your Lord do the two of you deny?
fa-bi-ayyi ala'i Rabbi-kuma tukadhdhiban. (55:33-36)

In the Name of Allah, the All-Merciful, the All-Compassionate
Bismi'llahi'r-Rahmani'r-Rahim

O Allah, I take refuge with You, and I seek access to You,
Allahumma inni a'udhu bi-ka wa atawassalu ilai-ka

and I direct myself toward You, and I address my humble entreaty to You,
wa atawajjahu ilai-ka wa atadarra'u ilai-ka

by invoking the Most Beautiful Names:
bi-Asma'i-ka'l-Husna.

He is Allah; there is no god but He (Majestic is His Majesty),
Huwa'llahu'lladhi la ilaha illa Hu (jalla jalalu-h)

the All-Merciful (Majestic is His Majesty),
ar-Rahmanu (jalla jalalu-h)

the All-Compassionate (Majestic is His Majesty),
ar-Rahimu (jalla jalalu-h)

the Sovereign Lord (Majestic is His Majesty),
al-Maliku (jalla jalalu-h)

the All-Holy (Majestic is His Majesty),
al-Quddusu (jalla jalalu-h)

the Source of Peace (Majestic is His Majesty),
as-Salamu (jalla jalalu-h)

the Safe-keeper (Majestic is His Majesty),
al-Mu'minu (jalla jalalu-h)

the Guardian (Majestic is His Majesty),
al-Muhaiminu (jalla jalalu-h)

the Almighty (Majestic is His Majesty),
al-'Azizu (jalla jalalu-h)

the All-Compelling (Majestic is His Majesty),
al-Jabbaru (jalla jalalu-h)

the Majestic (Majestic is His Majesty),
al-Mutakabbiru (jalla jalalu-h)

the Creator (Majestic is His Majesty),
al-Khaliqu (jalla jalalu-h)

the Maker (Majestic is His Majesty),
al-Bari'u (jalla jalalu-h)

the Shaper (Majestic is His Majesty),
al-Musawwiru (jalla jalalu-h)

the Forgiver (Majestic is His Majesty),
al-Ghaffaru (jalla jalalu-h)

the All-Prevailing
al-Qahharu (jalla jalalu-h)

the Bestower (Majestic is His Majesty),
al-Wahhabu (jalla jalalu-h)

the Provider (Majestic is His Majesty),
ar-Razzaqu (jalla jalalu-h)

the Opener (Majestic is His Majesty),
al-Fattahu (jalla jalalu-h)

the All-Knowing (Majestic is His Majesty),
al-'Alimu (jalla jalalu-h)

the Constrictor (Majestic is His Majesty),
al-Qabidu (jalla jalalu-h)

the Expander (Majestic is His Majesty),
al-Basitu (jalla jalalu-h)

the Abaser (Majestic is His Majesty),
al-Khafidu (jalla jalalu-h)

the Exalter (Majestic is His Majesty),
ar-Rafi'u (jalla jalalu-h)

the Honourer (Majestic is His Majesty),
al-Mu'izzu (jalla jalalu-h)

the Dishonourer (Majestic is His Majesty),
al-Mudhillu (jalla jalalu-h)

the All-Hearing (Majestic is His Majesty),
as-Sami'u (jalla jalalu-h)

the All-Seeing (Majestic is His Majesty),
al-Basiru (jalla jalalu-h)

the Judge (Majestic is His Majesty),
al-Hakamu (jalla jalalu-h)

the Just (Majestic is His Majesty),
al-'Adlu (jalla jalalu-h)

the Subtle (Majestic is His Majesty),
al-Latifu (jalla jālalu-h)

the Aware (Majestic is His Majesty),
al-Khabiru (jalla jalalu-h)

the Forbearing (Majestic is His Majesty),
al-Halimu (jalla jalalu-h) (Majestic is His Majesty),

the Magnificent (Majestic is His Majesty),
al-'Azimu (jalla jalalu-h)

the All-Forgiving (Majestic is His Majesty),
al-Ghafuru (jalla jalalu-h)

the Appreciative (Majestic is His Majesty),
ash-Shakuru (jalla jalalu-h)

the High, the Great (Majestic is His Majesty),
al-'Aliyyu'l-Kabiru (jalla jalalu-h)

the Preserver (Majestic is His Majesty),
al-Hafizu (jalla jalalu-h)

the Sustainer (Majestic is His Majesty),
al-Muqitu (jalla jalalu-h)

the Reckoner (Majestic is His Majesty),
al-Hasibu (jalla jalalu-h)

the Sublime (Majestic is His Majesty),
al-Jalilu (jalla jalalu-h)

the Generous (Majestic is His Majesty),
al-Karimu (jalla jalalu-h)

the Watchful (Majestic is His Majesty),
ar-Raqibu (jalla jalalu-h)

the Responsive (Majestic is His Majesty),
al-Mujibu (jalla jalalu-h)

the All-Embracing (Majestic is His Majesty),
al-Wasi'u (jalla jalalu-h)

the Wise (Majestic is His Majesty),
al-Hakimu (jalla jalalu-h)

the Loving (Majestic is His Majesty),
al-Wadudu (jalla jalalu-h)

the Glorious (Majestic is His Majesty),
al-Majidu (jalla jalalu-h)

the Resurrector (Majestic is His Majesty),
al-Ba'ithu (jalla jalalu-h)

the Witness (Majestic is His Majesty),
ash-Shahidu (jalla jalalu-h)

the Truth (Majestic is His Majesty),
al-Haqqu (jalla jalalu-h)

the Trustee (Majestic is His Majesty),
al-Wakilu (jalla jalalu-h)

the Strong (Majestic is His Majesty),
al-Qawiyyu (jalla jalalu-h)

the Firm (Majestic is His Majesty),
al-Matinu (jalla jalalu-h)

the Protecting Friend (Majestic is His Majesty),
al-Waliyyu (jalla jalalu-h)

the Praiseworthy (Majestic is His Majesty),
al-Hamidu (jalla jalalu-h)

the Reckoner (Majestic is His Majesty),
al-Muhsi (jalla jalalu-h)

the Originator (Majestic is His Majesty),
al-Mubdi'u (jalla jalalu-h)

the Restorer (Majestic is His Majesty),
al-Mu'idu (jalla jalalu-h)

the Giver of Life (Majestic is His Majesty),
al-Muhyi (jalla jalalu-h)

the Creator of Death (Majestic is His Majesty),
al-Mumitu (jalla jalalu-h)

the Ever-Living (Majestic is His Majesty),
al-Hayyu (jalla jalalu-h)

the Self-Subsisting (Majestic is His Majesty),
al-Qayyumu (jalla jalalu-h)

the Single (Majestic is His Majesty),
al-Wahidu (jalla jalalu-h)

the Noble (Majestic is His Majesty),
al-Majidu (jalla jalalu-h)

the One (Majestic is His Majesty),
al-Ahadu (jalla jalalu-h)

the Eternal (Majestic is His Majesty),
as-Samadu (jalla jalalu-h)

the All-Capable (Majestic is His Majesty),
al-Qadiru (jalla jalalu-h)

the All-Powerful (Majestic is His Majesty),
al-Muqtadiru (jalla jalalu-h)

the Accelerator (Majestic is His Majesty),
al-Muqaddimu (jalla jalalu-h)

the Delayer (Majestic is His Majesty),
al-Mu'akhkhiru (jalla jalalu-h)

the First (Majestic is His Majesty),
al-Awwalu (jalla jalalu-h)

the Last (Majestic is His Majesty),
al-Akhiru (jalla jalalu-h)

the Outer (Majestic is His Majesty),
az-Zahiru (jalla jalalu-h)

the Inner (Majestic is His Majesty),
al-Batinu (jalla jalalu-h)

the Governor (Majestic is His Majesty),
al-Wali (jalla jalalu-h)

the Exalted (Majestic is His Majesty),
al-Muta'ali (jalla jalalu-h)

the Source of Goodness (Majestic is His Majesty),
al-Birru (jalla jalalu-h)

the Acceptor of Repentance (Majestic is His Majesty),
at-Tawwabu (jalla jalalu-h)

the Benefactor (Majestic is His Majesty),
al-Mun'imu (jalla jalalu-h)

the Avenger (Majestic is His Majesty),
al-Muntaqimu (jalla jalalu-h)

the Pardoner (Majestic is His Majesty),
al-'Afuwwu (jalla jalalu-h)

the Kind (Majestic is His Majesty),
ar-Ra'ufu (jalla jalalu-h)

the Owner of Sovereignty (Majestic is His Majesty),
Maliku'l-Mulki (jalla jalalu-h)

the Owner of Majesty and Bounty (Majestic is His Majesty),
Dhu'l-Jalali wa'l-Ikrami (jalla jalalu-h)

the Lord (Majestic is His Majesty),
ar-Rabbu (jalla jalalu-h)

the Equitable (Majestic is His Majesty),
al-Muqsitu (jalla jalalu-h)

the Gatherer (Majestic is His Majesty),
al-Jami'u (jalla jalalu-h)

the Self-Sufficient (Majestic is His Majesty),
al-Ghaniyyu (jalla jalalu-h)

the Enricher (Majestic is His Majesty),
al-Mughni (jalla jalalu-h)

the Giver (Majestic is His Majesty),
al-Mu'ti (jalla jalalu-h)

the Withholder (Majestic is His Majesty),
al-Mani'u (jalla jalalu-h)

the Distresser (Majestic is His Majesty),
ad-Zarru (jalla jalalu-h)

the Beneficent (Majestic is His Majesty),
an-Nafi'u (jalla jalalu-h)

the Light (Majestic is His Majesty),
an-Nuru (jalla jalalu-h)

the Guide (Majestic is His Majesty),
al-Hadi (jalla jalalu-h)

the Incomparable (Majestic is His Majesty),
al-Badi'u (jalla jalalu-h)

the Everlasting (Majestic is His Majesty),
al-Baqi (jalla jalalu-h)

the Inheritor (Majestic is His Majesty),
al-Warithu (jalla jalalu-h)

the Director (Majestic is His Majesty),
ar-Rashidu (jalla jalalu-h)

the Ever-Patient (Majestic is His Majesty),
as-Saburu (jalla jalalu-h)

He is Allah, the Single, the One, the Unique, the Eternal,
Huwa'llahu'l-Wahidu'l-Ahadu'l-Fardu's-Samadu'lladhi

who has taken for Himself no consort and no son.
lam yattadhikh sahibatan wa la walada

He does not beget, nor was He begotten;
lam yalid wa lam yulad :

and there is none comparable unto Him.
wa lam yakun la-hu kufuwan ahad. (112:3-4)

His are the Most Beautiful Names.
la-hu'l-asma'u'l-husna. (20:8)

-and the most exalted attributes.
-wa's-sifatu'l-'ulya

His is the Supreme Analogy in the heavens and the earth.
wa la-hu'l-Mathalu'l-A'la fi's-samawati wa'l-ard :

He is the Almighty, the All-Wise.
wa Huwa'l-'Azizu'l-Hakim. (30:27)

There is nothing like unto Him, and He is
laisa ka-mithli-hi shai' :

the All-Hearing, the All-Seeing.
wa Huwa's-Sam,'u'l-Basir. (42:11)

The eyes do not perceive Him, but He perceives the eyes.
la tudriku-hu'l-absaru wa Huwa yudriku'l-absar :

He is the Subtle, the Aware.
wa Huwa'l-Latifu'l-Khabir. (6:103)

He is the First and the Last, the Outer and the Inner.
Huwa'l-Awwalu wa'l-Akhiru wa'z-Zahiru wa'l-Batin :

He is Aware of all things.
wa Huwa bi-kulli shai'in' Alim. (57:3)

Say: "We believe in Allah and what is sent down
qulu amanna bi'llahi wa ma unzila

to us, and what was sent down to Abraham,
ilai-na wa ma unzila ila Ibrahima

and Ishmael, and Isaac, and Jacob, and the tribes,
wa Isma'ila wa Ishaqa wa Ya'quba

and that which Moses and Jesus received, and that
wa'l-asbati wa ma utiya Musa wa'Isa

which the Prophets received from their Lord.
wa ma utiya'n-Nabiyyuna min Rabbi-him :

We make no distinction between any of them,
la nufarriqu baina ahadin min-hum

and to Him we have surrendered."
wa nahnu la-hu muslimun. (2:136)

Our Lord, we believe in what You have revealed
Rabba-na amanna bi-ma anzalta

and we follow the Messenger.
wa'ttaba'na'r-Rasula

so enroll us among those who witness.
fa-'ktub-na ma'a'sh-shahidin. (3:53)

We believe in Allah, and His Angels, and His Books,
amanna bi'llahi wa Mala'ikati-hi wa Kutubi-hi

and His Messengers, and the Last Day,
wa Rusuli-hi wa'l-Yawmi'l-Akhiri

and that Destiny-both the good of it and the bad of it,
wa'l-Qadari khairi-hi wa sharri-hi

and both its sweetness and its bitterness-
wa hulwi-hi wa murri-hi

is from Allah (Exalted is He).
mina'llahi (ta'ala)

Our Lord, we believe in You,
Rabba-na amanna bi-ka

and in Your Names and Your attributes,
wa bi-Asma'i-ka wa sifati-ka

and in whatever is ascribed to You in the Exaltation of Your Essence,
wa ma Anta bi-hi mawsufun fi'Uluwwi Dhati-ka

as befits the Majesty of Your Countenance,
ka-ma yanbaghi li-Jalali Wajhi-ka

and of which You are Worthy in the Splendour of Your Lordliness,
wa ma Anta la-hu Ahlun fi'Azimi Rububiyyati-ka

and as is appropriate to You in the Perfection of Your Divinity.
wa ka-ma huwa'l-la'iqu bi-ka fi Kamali Uluhiyyati-k.

We believe in You, and Your Books and Your Messengers,
amanna bi-ka wa bi-Kutubi-ka wa Rusuli-ka

and in Muhammad (Allah bless him and give him peace),
wa bi-Muhammadin (salla'llahu 'alai-hi wa sallam)

Your servant and Your Messenger,
'abdi-ka wa Rasuli-ka

and in what he has brought from Your Presence,
wa bi-ma ja'a bi-hi min 'Indi-ka

and [we do so] in accordance with Your Purpose
wa'ala muradi-ka

and the purpose of Your Messengers,
wa muradi Rusuli-ka

as You love and approve, and in accordance
wa ka-ma tuhibbu wa tarda

with what is within Your Knowledge Most High.
wa'ala ma huwa fi'Ilmi-ka'l-A'la.

O Knower of the secret and that which is more deeply hidden still!
ya'Alima's-sirri wa akhfa.

O Sustainer of the earth and the sky!
ya Qayyuma'l-ardi wa's-sama'.

O Allah, we are incompetent, inadequate,
Allahumma inna'ajizuna qasiruna

turning to You from deviation and error,
bira'un ilai-ka mina'z-zaighi wa'z-zalali

as we try to obey what You have commanded, in word and deed and action.

min qawlin wa fi'lin wa'amal.

Now Allah be Exalted, the True King!
fa-ta'ala'llahu Maliku'l-Haqq :

There is no god but He, the Lord of the Throne of Grace.
la ilaha illa Hu: Rabbu'l-'arshi'l-karim. (23:116)

Glory be to Him! High Exalted be He
subhana-hu wa ta'ala

above what they attribute [to Him]! (6:100)
'amma yasifun. (6:100)

The Originator of the heavens and the earth!
Badi'u's-samawati wa'l-ard :

How can He have a child, when there is for Him no consort,
anna yakunu la-hu waladun wa lam takun la-hu sahiba :

when He created all things and is Aware of all things.
wa khalaqa kulla shai': wa Huwa bi-kulli shai'in'Alim. (6:101)

O Allah, cause us to live in accordance with that,
Allahumma fa-ahyi-na'ala dhalik.

and cause us to die in accordance with that.
wa amit-na'ala dhalik.

and restore us to life in accordance with that,
wa'b'ath-na'ala dhalik.

and guide us to the realities of that.
wa'hdi-na li-haqa'iqi dhalik.

O Lord of All the Worlds!

ya Rabba'l-'alamin.

O He who is the First, before all things,
ya man Huwa'l-Awwalu qabla kulli shai'in

and the Last, after all things,
wa'l-Akhiru ba'da kulli shai'.

and the Outer, above all things,
wa'z-Zahiru fawqa kulli shai'.

and the Inner, below all things,
wa'l-Batinu duna kulli shai'.

and the Irresistible, above all things.
wa'l-Qahiru fawqa kulli shai'.

O Light of lights! O Knower of the mysteries!
ya Nura'l-anwari ya'Alima'l-asrar.

O Controller of the night and the day!
ya Mudabbira'l-laili wa'n-nahar.

O Sovereign Lord, O Almighty One, O All-Prevailing One!
ya Maliku ya'Azizu ya Qahhar.

O All-Compassionate One, O Ever-Loving One, O All Forgiving One!
ya Rahimu ya Wadudu ya Ghaffar

O Knower of the invisible realms.
ya'Allama'l-ghuyub.

O Transformer of hearts!
ya Muqalliba'l-qulub.

O Veiler of faults! O Forgiver of sins!
ya Sattara'l-'uyub. ya Ghaffara'dh-dhunub.

O Allah, bless our master Muhammad, Your servant
Allahumma salli 'ala sayyidi-na Muhammadin 'abdi-ka

and Your Messenger, the perfect master, the opener, the seal,
wa Rasuli-ka's-sayyidi'l-kamili'l-fatihi'l-khatimi

Your clear Light, and Your truthful and trustworthy Messenger.
nuri-ka'l-mubin wa Rasuli-ka's-sadiqi'l-amin.

O Allah, grant him excellent merit,
Allahumma wa ati-hi'l-fadilata

and means of access and intercession.
wa'l-wasilata wa'sh-shafa'a.

Bestow upon him the praiseworthy station
wa'b'ath-hu'l-maqama'l-mahmuda'lladhi

that You have promised him, the approved intercessor
wa'adta-hu'sh-shafi'i'l-murtada

and the chosen Prophet.
wa'r-Rasuli'l-mujtaba.

O Allah, bless him and his family,
Allahumma salli 'alai-hi wa'ala ali-hi

as You have blessed Abraham and the family of Abraham.
ka-ma sallaita'ala Ibrahima wa'ala ali Ibrahima

Bestow grace upon Muhammad and the family of Muhammad,
wa barik 'ala Muhammadin wa'ala ali Muhammadin

as You have bestowed grace upon Abraham
ka-ma barakta 'ala Ibrahima

and the family of Abraham, in all the worlds.
wa'ala ali Ibrahima fi'l-'alamina

You are Praiseworthy, Glorious,
inna-ka Hamidun Majidun

to the extent of the number of Your creatures,
'adada khalqi-ka

the good pleasure of Your Own Self,
wa rida'a Nafsi-ka

the weight of Your Throne, and the ink of Your Words.
wa zinata 'Arshi-ka wa midadi kalimati-ka

And bless his family and his Companions, one and all,
wa'ala ali-hi wa sahbi-hi ajma'ina

and grant them much peace.
wa sallim tasliman kathira.

O Allah, we appeal to You by invoking Your most beautiful Names,
Allahumma inna nas'alu-ka bi-Asma'i-ka'l-Husna

and Your most exalted Attributes, and Your perfect Words,
wa sifati-ka'l-'ulya wa kalimati-ka't-tammati

and Your revealed Scriptures and Your glorious Book,
wa kutubi-ka'l-munzalati wa bi-kitabi-ka'l-'azizi

and our master Muhammad (Allah bless him and give him peace),

wa bi-sayyidi-na Muhammadin (salla'llahu 'alai-hi wa sallam)

Your servant and Your Messenger.
'abdi-ka wa Rasuli-ka

O Lord of lords! O Revealer of the Book! O Swift in reckoning!
ya Rabba'l-arbab: ya Munazzila'l-Kitab: ya Sari'a'l-hisab:

O He who responds when He is called upon!
ya man idha du'iya ajab.

O All-Compassionate, O All-Merciful!
ya Rahimu ya Rahman:

O Ever-Near, O Responsive One!
ya Qaribu ya Mujibu ya Hannanu ya Mannanu

O Tender One, O Benefactor!
ya Hannanu ya Mannan:

O Lord of Majesty and Honour!
ya Dha'l-Jalali wa'l-Ikram:

O Ever-Living One, O Self-Sustaining One!
ya Hayyu ya Qayyum.

"Our Lord, give us in this world that which is good,
Rabba-na ati-na fi'd-dunya hasanatan

and in the Hereafter that which is good,
wa fi'l-akhirati hasanatan

and guard us against the torment of the Fire [of Hell]."
wa qi-na'adhaba'n-nar. (2:201)

O Allah, we appeal to You for guidance,
Allahumma inna nas'alu-ka'l-huda

and pious devotion, and chastity, and sufficiency.
wa't-tuqa wa'l-'afafa wa'l-ghina

We take refuge with You from the strain of tribulation,
wa na'udhu bi-ka min jahdi'l-bala'i

and the impact of misfortune, and the evil of fate,
wa darki'sh-shaqa'i wa su'i'l-qada'i

and the malice of enemies.
wa shamati'l-a'da'.

O Allah, we ask You for that which is good, for all of it,
Allahumma inna nas'alu-ka mina'l-khairi kulli-hi

both that which is immediate and that which is delayed.
'ajili-hi wa ajili-h.

We take refuge with You from that which is evil, from all of it,
wa na'udhu bi-ka mina'sh-sharri kulli-hi

both that which is immediate and that which is delayed,
'ajili-hi wa ajili-hi

both that which we know and that which we do not know.
ma'alimna min-hu wa ma lam na'lam.

Praise be to You, for You are the One of whom help is sought,
la-ka'l-hamdu wa Anta'l-Musta'anu

and reliance is placed on You.
wa'alai-ka't-tuklan.

There is no power and no strength except through You.
wa la hawla wa la quwwata illa bi-k.

O Allah, we ask You for goodness like that asked of You
Allahumma inna nas'alu-ka min khairin ma sa'ala-ka min-hu

by Your servant and Your Prophet, our master Muhammad
'abdu-ka wa Nabiyyu-ka sayyidu-na Muhammadun

(Allah bless him and give him peace).
(salla'llahu 'alai-hi wa sallam).

O Allah, You are my Lord. There is no god but You.
Allahumma Anta Rabbi la ilaha illa Anta

You have created me, and I am committed to Your covenant
wa ana'abdu-ka wa ana'ala'ahdi-ka

and Your promise, as far as I am able.
wa wa'di-ka ma'stata't.

I take refuge with You from the evil I have done,
a'udhu bi-ka min sharri ma sana'tu

and I acknowledge Your gracious favour bestowed upon me,
wa abu'u la-ka bi-ni'mati-ka'alayya

and I confess my sin, so forgive me my sins,
wa abu'u bi-dhanbi fa-'ghfir li dhunubi

for no one forgives sins except You.
fa-inna-hu la yaghfiru'dh-dhunuba illa Anta

O All-Forgiving One! O All-Forgiving One!
ya Ghafuru ya Ghafuru

O All-Forgiving One! O All-Forgiving One!
ya Ghafuru ya Ghafur.

WIRD AS-SUBH – 2

O Allah, I appeal to You for the companionship of fear,
Allahumma inni as'alu-ka suhbata'l-khawfi

and the rapture of ardent longing,
wa ghalabata'sh-shawqi

and the certainty of knowledge, and the constancy of reflection.
wa thabata'l-'ilmi wa dawama'l-fikr.

We appeal to You, by invoking
wa nas'alu-ka

the secret of secrets, which protects from all kinds of harm,
bi-sirri'l-asrari'l-mani'i mina'l-adrari

so that sins and faults may have no permanent lodging with us.
hatta la yakuna la-na ma'a'dh-dhunubi wa'l-'uyubi qarar.

Make our footing firm, and guide us to knowledge and practice,
wa thabbit-na wa'hdi-na li'l-'ilmi wa'l-'amali

and adorn us with these words, which You set forth
wa zayyin-na bi-hadhihi'l-kalimati'llati basatta-ha

upon the tongue of Your Messenger Muhammad
'ala lisani Rasuli-ka Muhammadin

(Allah bless him and give him peace),
(salla'llahu 'alai-hi wa sallam)

and with which You tested Abraham,
wa'btalaita bi-hinna Ibrahima

Your Bosom Friend (peace be upon him),
Khalila-ka ('alai-his-salam)

for You fulfilled them and You said:
fa-átamma-hunna fa-qulta:

"Behold, I am making you a leader for the people." [Abraham] said:
inni ja'ilu-ka li-'n-nasi imama :

'And [making leaders] of my offspring?' [His Lord] said:
qala wa min dhurriyyati :

'My covenant does not extend to the evildoers.'"
qala la yanalu'ahdi'z-zalimin. (2:124)

Include us, therefore, among those who are active in goodness,
fa-'j'al-na mina'l-muhsinina

among his offspring and the offspring of Adam and Noah.
min dhurriyyati-hi wa min dhurriyyati Adama wa Nuh.

I also beg You, O Allah, to show us the way of the righteous leaders,
wa as'alu-ka Allahumma bi-na sabila a'immati'l-muttaqina

in the Name of Allah, and from Allah, and toward Allah.
bi'smi'llahi wa mina'llahi wa ila'llah.

In Allah the believers put their trust.
wa'ala'llahi fa-l'-yatawakkili'l-mu'minun. (3:122)

Allah is enough for me.
hasbiya'llahu (9:129)

I believe in Allah. I am content with Allah. I have put my trust in Allah.
amantu bi'llah: raditu bi'llah: tawakkaltu'ala'llah.

There is no power and no strength except with Allah.
la hawla wa la quwwata illa bi'llah.

"There is no god but You. Glory be to You!
la ilaha illa Anta subhana-ka

I have been an evildoer."
inni kuntu mina'z-zalimin. (21:87)

O All-High! O Magnificent One! O Forbearing One!
ya'Aliyyu ya'Azimu ya Halimu

O All-Knowing One! O All-Hearing One! O All-Seeing One!
ya'Alimu ya Sami'u ya Basiru

O Supportive One! O All-Capable One!
ya Mu'ayyidu ya Qadiru

O Ever-Living One! O Self-Sustaining One!
ya Hayyu ya Qayyumu

O All-Merciful! O All-Compassionate!
ya Rahmanu ya Rahimu

O He who is He, He, He! O He!

ya man Huwa Huwa Huwa ya Hu

O First! O Last! O Outer! O Inner!
ya Awwalu ya Akhiru ya Zahiru ya Batin.

Blessed be the Name of your Lord,
tabaraka'smu Rabbi-ka

the Owner of Majesty and Honour.
Dhi'l-Jalali wa'l-Ikram. (55:78)

O Allah, guide us with Your light toward You,
Allahumma'hdi-na bi-nuri-ka ilai-ka

and make us stand in genuine servitude before You.
wa aqim-na bi-sidqi'l-'ubudiyyati baina yadai-k.

O Allah, make our tongues moist with Your remembrance,
Allahumma'j 'al alsinata-na ratbatan bi-dhikri-ka

and our lower selves obedient to Your command,
wa nufusa-na muti'atan li-amri-ka

and our hearts full of Your intimate knowledge,
wa quluba-na mamlu'atan bi-ma'rifati-ka

and our spirits honoured by the direct vision of You,
wa arwaha-na mukarramatan bi-mushahadati-ka

and our innermost beings blessed by Your nearness.
wa'rzuq-na fi dunya-ka wa mazidan ladai-ka

Grant us sustenance in this world, and yet more in Your presence, for You are indeed Capable of all things.
inna-ka'ala kulli shai'in Qadir.

O He without whose nearness and permanence no heart can be at rest,
ya man la yaskunu qalbun illa bi-qurbi-hi wa qarari-hi

and without whose tender grace and kindness no servant can live,
wa la yahya'abdun illa bi-lutfi-hi wa ibrari-hi

and without whose support and assistance no being can survive!
wa la yabqa wujudun illa bi-imdadi-hi wa izhari-h.

O He who befriends His righteous servants,
ya man anasa'ibada-hu'l-abrar:

and His most excellent saints drawn near,
wa awliya'a-hu'l-muqarrabina'l-akhyar:

with His intimate converse and His secrets!
bi-munajati-hi wa asrari-h.

O He who causes death and brings to life,
ya man amata wa ahya

and sends far away and brings near,
wa aqsa wa adna

and causes happiness and misery,
wa as'ada wa ashqa

and sends astray and guides aright,
wa adalla wa hada

and impoverishes and enriches,
wa afqara wa aghna

and afflicts and restores to well-being,
wa abla wa'afa

and determines and gives judgment!
wa qaddara wa qada

Everything is subject to the splendid grace
kullun bi-'azimi lutfi

of His management and His predestination.
tadbiri-hi wa sabiqi iqdari-h.

My Lord, what doorway should I approach, apart from Your doorway,
Rabbi ayya babin aqsudu ghaira babi-ka

and in what direction should I face, apart from Your direction?
wa ayya janabin atawajjahu ghaira janaba-k.

You are the All-High, the Magnificent,
Anta'l-'Aliyyu'l-'Azim.

There is no power and no strength except with You.
la hawla wa la quwwata la-na illa bi-k.

My Lord, whom should I approach,
Rabbi ila man aqsudu

when You are the Lord to be approached,
wa Anta'r-Rabbu'l-maqsudu

and to whom should I direct my attention,
wa ila man atawajjahu

when You are the Truth to be worshipped?

wa Anta'l-Haqqu'l-Ma'bud.

Who is there to give to me,
wa man dha'lladhi yu'ti-ni

when You are the Owner of generosity and magnanimity?
wa Anta Sahibu'l-karami wa'l-jud.

My Lord, it is not right for me to complain to anyone but You,
Rabbi haqiqun'alayya an la ashtakiya illa ilai-ka

and it is not proper for me to put my trust in anyone but You.
wa lazimun'alayya an la atawakkala illa'alai-k.

O He in whom the trusting put their trust!
ya man'alai-hi yatawakkalu'l-mutawakkiluna

O He to whom the fearful turn for refuge!
ya man ilai-hi yalja'u'l-kha'ifun.

O He on whose generosity and beautiful customs the hopeful depend!
ya man bi-karami-hi wa jamili'awa'idi-hi yata'allaqu'r-rajun.

O He to whose irresistible authority, and splendid mercy
ya man bi-sultani qahri-hi wa'azimi rahmati-hi

and tender kindness, the suffering appeal for help!
wa birri-hi yastaghithu'l-mudtarruna

O He to whose abundant giving,
ya man li-wus'i'ata'i-hi

and gracious favour and blessed bounty,
wa jamili fadli-hi wa na'ma'i-hi

hands are outstretched and beggars address their appeal!
tubsatu'l-aidi wa yas'alu-hu's-sa'iluna

My Lord, include me among those who put their trust in You,
Rabbi'j 'al-ni mim-man tawakkala 'alai-ka

and set my fear to rest when I attain to You,
wa amin khawfi idha wasaltu ilai-ka

and do not disappoint my hope when I come to be in Your presence.
wa la tukhayyib raja'i idha sirtu baina yadai-k.

O Ever-Near One, O Responsive One, O All-Hearing One!
ya Qaribu ya Mujibu ya Sami'.

O Allah, we are wandering astray, so guide us,
Allahumma inna dalluna fa-'hdi-na

and we are poor, so enrich us, and we are weak, so strengthen us,
wa inna fuqara'u fa-aghni-na wa inna du'afa'u fa-qawwi-na.

and we are sinners, so forgive us.
wa inna mudhnibuna fa-'ghfir la-na

O Light, O Guide, O Independent One, O Strong One!
ya Nuru ya Hadi ya Ghaniyyu ya Qawiyy.

O All-Forgiving, O All-Compassionate One!
ya Ghafuru ya Rahim.

O Allah, with a spirit from Your presence support us,
Allahumma bi-ruhin min'indi-ka ayyid-na

and from Your hidden knowledge instruct us,

wa min'ilmi-ka'l-maknuni'allim-na

and to Your religion that You have approved
wa'ala dini-ka'lladhi'rtadaita-hu

make us firmly committed,
habbit-na

and include us among those to whom the fairest reward-
wa'j'al-na mim-man sabaqat la-hu

and more besides-has already gone forth.
min-ka'l-husna wa ziyada.

O Allah, I appeal to You in this world for obedience to You
Allahumma inni as'alu-ka fi'd-dunya ta'ata-ka

and for escape from disobedience to You,
wa'l-firara'an ma'siyati-ka

and in the Hereafter for Your Garden of Paradise,
wa fi'l-akhirati jannata-ka

and for the vision of You, and for immunity from Your chastisement.
wa ru'yata-ka wa's-salamata min'uqubati-k.

O Allah, let us live as obedient believers,
Allahumma ahyi-na mu'minina ta'i'ina

and let us die as penitent Muslims.
wa tawaffa-na muslimina ta'ibin.

Include us among those who receive their record with the right hand, wa'j'al-na mim-man ya'khudhu'l-kitaba bi'l-yamin.

and cause us to be safe on the Day of the Greatest Alarm.
wa'j'al-na yawma'l-faza'i'l-akbari aminin.

Set our feet firmly on the straight path,
wa thabbit aqdama-na'ala's-sirati'l-mustaqim.

and admit us into Your mercy and Your noble generosity
wa adkhil-na bi-rahmati-ka wa karami-ka

in the Gardens of Bliss,
fi jannati'n-na'im.

and deliver us, through Your pardon and Your forbearance,
wa najji-na bi-'afwi-ka wa hilmi-ka

from the painful torment.
mina'l-'adhabi'l-alim.

O Munificent One, O All-Compassionate,
ya Barru ya Rahimu

O All-Forbearing, O Generous One!
ya Halimu ya Karimu.

O Allah, we have come to the point where we possess for ourselves
Allahumma inna asbahna la namliku li-anfusi-na

no defence and no remission, no means to cause harm
daf'an wa la raf'an wa la darran

and no source of benefit.
la naf'an

We are paupers, with nothing belonging to us,
inna fuqara'u la shai'a la-na

and weaklings, with no strength of our own.
dufa'a'u la quwwata la-na

All goodness has come to be in Your hands,
wa asbaha'l-khairu kullu-hu bi-yadai-ka

and the ordering of everything is reverting to You.
wa amru kulli shai'in raji'un ilai-k.

O Allah, enable us to do what You have commanded us to do.
Allahumma waffiq-na li-ma bi-hi amarta-na.

Help us to perform the duties You have imposed upon us,
wa a'in-na'ala ma bi-hi kallafta-na

and make us independent of all things,
wa aghni-na'an kulli shai'in

through Your gracious favour and Your merciful compassion.
bi-fadli-ka wa rahmati-ka

Mend what is broken for us, and restore what we have lost,
wa'jbur kasra-na wa ma fata min-na

through Your providential care and Your noble generosity.
bi-'inayati-ka wa karami-ka

Assist us to direct our attention toward You,
wa ayyid-na bi't-tawajjuhi ilai-ka

by means of Your power and Your strength.
bi-hawli-ka wa quwwati-ka ya Maliku

O Sovereign Lord, O Omnipotent One!
ya Sami'u ya Basir.

O All-Hearing One, O All-Seeing One! O Allah, our sight has not failed to see,
Allahumma ma qasara'an-hu ra'yu-na

nor has our asking failed to obtain,
wa lam tablugh-hu mas'alatu-na

whatever goodness You have promised to any one of Your creatures,
min khairin wa'adta-hu ahadan min khalqi-k.

or whatever goodness You are giving to any one of Your servants.
aw khairin Anta Mu'ti-hi ahadan min'ibadi-k.

We therefore seek it from You and ask it of You,
fa-inna narghabu ilai-ka fi-hi wa nas'alu-ka-hu

through Your mercy, O Most Merciful of the merciful.
bi-rahmati-ka ya Arhama'r-Rahimin.

O Allah, I complain to You about the feebleness of my strength,
Allahumma inni ashku ilai-ka da'fa quwwati

the paucity of my skill, and my insignificance in the eyes of creatures.
wa qillata hilati wa hawani'ala'l-makhluqin.

You are the Most Merciful of the merciful.
wa Anta Arhamu'r-Rahimin.

You are the Lord of those who are considered weak.

Anta Rabbu'l-mustad'afin.

You are my Lord. To whom would You entrust me?
wa Anta Rabbi ila man takilu-ni

To someone remote, who would shun me,
ila ba'idin yatahajjamu-ni

or to an enemy, whom You had put in charge of my affair?
am ila'aduwwin mallakta-hu amri.

If there is no anger against me from You, I am not worried,
in lam yakun'alayya ghadabun min-ka fa-la ubali

but Your pardon is what matters to me most.
wa lakin'afwu-ka awsa'u li.

I take refuge with the Light of Your Countenance,
a'udhu bi-nuri Wajhi-ka'lladhi

by which the darknesses are illumined,
ashraqat bi-hi'z-zulumatu

and by which the business of this world and the Hereafter
wa saluha'alai-hi amru'd-dunya wa'l-akhirati

is saved from having Your anger descend upon it,
min an yanzila'alayya ghadabu-ka

or Your displeasure alighting upon me.
aw yahilla'alayya sakhatu-k.

Praise be to You, until You are well pleased.
la-ka'l-hamdu hatta tarda.

We have no power and no strength except through You.

wa la hawla wa la quwwata la-na illa bi-k.

My Lord, I complain to You about the fickleness
Rabbi inni ashku ilai-ka talawwuna

of my spiritual states and the hesitancy of my request.
ahwali wa tawaqqufa su'ali.

O He on the grace of whose generosity,
ya man ta'allaqat bi-lutfi karami-hi

and on the beauty of whose customs, my hopes depend!
wa jamili 'awa'idi-hi amali

O He from whom my condition is not concealed!
ya man la yakhfa'alai-hi khafiyyu hali.

O He who knows the outcome of my business, and what my end will be!
ya man ya'lamu 'aqibata amri wa ma'ali.

My Lord, my forelock is in Your hands,
Rabbi inna nasiyati bi-yadai-ka

and all my affairs are returning to You.
Rabbi inna nasiyati bi-yadai-ka wa umuri kullu-ha raji'atun ilai-k.

My spiritual states are not concealed from You,
wa ahwali la takhfa 'alai-k.

and my cares and sorrows are well known to You.
wa humumi wa ahzani ma'lumatun ladai-k.

My affliction is great, and tremendous is my grief,

qad jalla musabi wa'azuma'kti'abi.

and my youth is past and gone,
wa'nsarama shababi

and my pure drink has turned muddy,
wa takaddara'alayya safwu sharabi

and my cares and my agonies have gathered against me,
wa'jtama'at 'alayya humumi wa awsabi

and the prompt fulfilment of my wish has been delayed,
wa ta'akhkhara 'an-ni ta'jilu matlabi

along with the clearing of my blame and my censure.
wa tanjizu i'tabi wa'itabi.

O He to whom is my return and my homeward journey!
ya man ilai-hi marji'i wa ma'abi.

O He who hears and knows the thoughts of my innermost being,
ya man yasma'u wa ya'lamu hawajisa sirri

as well as my public statements, and who knows
wa 'alaniyyata khitabi wa ya'lamu

the nature of my hope and the reality of my condition.
mahiyyata amali wa haqiqata ma bi.

My God, my power is inadequate, and my skill is slight,
Ilahi qad'ajazat qudrati wa qallat hilati

and my strength is weak, and my mind is wandering,
wa da'ufat quwwati wa tahat fikrati

and my problem is difficult, and my spiritual state is bad,
wa ashkalat qadiyyati wa sa'at halati

and my wish is far from fulfilment,
wa ba'udat umniyati

and my distress is tremendous,
wa'azumat hasrati

and my moaning grows ever louder,
wa tasa'adat zafrati

and the hidden content of my innermost being is exposed,
wa'ttadaha maknunu sarirati

and my significance has melted away.
wa salat'ibrati.

You are my refuge and my means of access.
wa Anta malja'i wa wasilati

To You I offer my sorrow, my sadness and my complaint,
wa ilai-ka arfa'u baththi wa huzni wa shikayati

and I pin my hope on You for the dispelling of my misfortunes.
wa arju-ka li-daf'i mulimmati.

O He who knows my innermost secret and my public statement.
ya man ya'lamu sirri wa'alaniyati.

My God, Your door is open to the beggar,
Ilahi babu-ka maftuhun li's-sa'il:

and Your gracious favour is freely dispensed to the visitor, wa fadlu-ka mabdhulun li'n-na'il:

and to You is the final notice of complaint
wa ilai-ka muntaha'sh-shakwa

and the ultimate delivery of questions.
wa ghayatu'l-masa'il.

My God, have mercy on my pleading tears,
Ilahi'rham dam'iya's-sa'ila

and my shrivelled body, and my languid state,
wa jismiya'n-nahila

and my declining youth.
wa shababiya'l-ma'il.

O He to whom complaints are raised!
ya man ilai-hi raf'u'sh-shakwa

O Knower of the secret and the private conversation!
Ya 'Alima's-sirri wa'n-najwa.

O He who hears and sees,
ya man yasma'u wa yara.

and O He who is at the highest observation post!
ya man Huwa bi'l-manzari'l-a'la.

O Lord of the earth and the sky!
ya Rabba'l-ardi wa's-sama.

O He to whom the Most Beautiful Names belong!
ya man la-hu'l-Asma' al-Husna.

O He to whom permanence and everlastingness belong!

ya man la-hu'd-dawamu wa'l-baqa.

O my Lord, Your servant is short of material means,
ya Rabbi'abdu-ka qad daqat bi-hi'l-asbab:

and the doors are shut in his face,
wa ghulliqat duna-hu'l-abwab:

and it is hard for him to follow the path of the people of righteousness,
wa ta'adhdhara 'alai-hi suluku tariqi ahli's-sawab:

and he experiences increasing care and sorrow and grief,
wa zada bi-hi'l-hammu wa'l-ghammu wa'l-ikti'ab:

and his life is almost over, and no door has been opened
wa'nqada'umru-hu wa lam yuftah la-hu

to admit him to the clarity of those blissful situations,
ila fasihi tilka'l-hadarati

nor to the fountains of purity and comfort.
wa manahili's-safwi wa'r-rahati bab.

His days have slipped away,
wa'nsaramat ayyamu-hu

and the lower self is grazing in the arenas of heedlessness
wa'n-nafsu ra'i'atun fi mayadini'l-ghaflati

and earning a livelihood worthy of contempt.
wa daniyyi'l-iktisab.

You are the One of whom the removal of this disaster is sought.
wa Anta'l-Marjuwwu li-kashfi hadha'l-musab.

O He who always answers when appeal is made to Him!
ya man idha du'iya ajab.

O Swift in reckoning! O Lord of lords!
ya Sari'a'l-hisab: ya Rabba'l-arbab.

O Magnificent in Dignity!
Ya 'Azima'l-Janab.

O Generous One, O Bestower of gifts!
ya Karimu ya Wahhab.

My Lord, do not exclude my supplication,
Rabbi la tahjub da'wati.

and do not reject my request,
wa la tarudda mas'alati.

and do not leave me in my distress,
wa la tada'-ni bi-hasrati.

and do not entrust me to my own power and my own strength,
wa la takil-ni ila hawli wa quwwati.

but have mercy on my incompetence and my need,
wa'rham'ajzi wa faqati.

for my breast is tight, my mind is wandering,
fa-qad daqa sadri wa taha fikri

and I am confused about my state of affairs.
wa tahayyartu fi amri

You are the Knower of my secret and my public statement,
wa Anta'l-'Alimu bi-sirri wa jahri:

the Master of my benefit and what is harmful to me,
al-Maliku li-naf'i wa durri:

the One who is Capable of cheering my sorrow and easing my hardship.
al-Qadiru'ala tafriji karbi wa taisiri'usri.

My Lord, have mercy on him whose sickness is serious,
Rabbi'rham man'azuma maradu-hu

and whose cure is hard to find,
wa'azza shifa'u-hu

and whose illness is considerable though his treatment is slight,
wa kathura da'u-hu wa qalla dawa'u-hu

and whose skill is weak though his affliction is strong.
wa qawiya bala'u-h.

You are his refuge, and his hope, and his help and his healing
wa Anta malju'u-hu wa raja'u-hu wa'awnu-hu wa shifa'u-h.

O He whose gracious favour and gifts have inundated His servants,
ya man ghamara'l-'ibada fadlu-hu wa'ata'u-h:

and whose generosity and beneficence have embraced the universe.
wa wasi'a'l-bariyyata judu-hu wa na'ma'u-h.

Here am I, Your servant in need of what is in Your presence,
ha ana'abdu-ka muhtajun ila ma'inda-k:

a pauper, awaiting Your munificence and Your gift;

faqirun antziru juda-ka wa rifda-k:

a sinner, begging You for pardon and forgiveness,
mudhnibun as'alu min-ka'l-'afwa wa'l-ghufran.

fearfully seeking from You exemption and security;
kha'ifun atlubu min-ka's-safha wa'l-aman.

a wicked rebel, though maybe repentance will erase
musiyyun'asin fa-'asa tawbatun

the darkness of wickedness and rebellion;
tamhu zulma'l-isa'ati wa'l-'isyan.

a beggar, extending the hands of total need;
sa'ilun basitun yadayi'l-faqati'l-kulliyyati

looking to You for generosity and beneficence;
yatlubu min-ka'l-juda wa'l-ihsan.

a prisoner bound, yet maybe his chains will be broken,
masjunun muqayyadun fa-'asa yufakku qaidu-h.

and he will be released from the jail of his confinement,
wa yutlaqu min sijni hijabi-hi

into the clear scenes of witnessing, and the fountains;
ila fasihi hadarati'sh-shuhudi wa'l-a'yan:

naked and hungry, yet maybe he will be nourished
ja'i 'un 'arin fa-'asa yut 'amu

with the drink of bringing near,
min sharabi't-taqrib.

and clothed with the garments of faith;

wa yuksa min hulali'l-iman:

thirsty, thirsty, and O so thirsty,
zam'an: zam'an: wa ayyu zam'an.

he is burning in the bowels of the blazing fires,
yata'ajjaju fi ahsha'i-hi lahibu'n-niran:

yet maybe the fires of grief will be cooled for him,
fa-'asa an tabruda'an-hu niranu'l-karb:

and his thirst will be quenched with the drink of love,
wa yusqa min sharabi'l-hubb:

and he will sip from the cups of nearness,
wa yakra'a min kasati'l-qurb:

and the suffering and the pains will leave him,
wa yadhhaba 'an-hu'l-bu'su wa'l-alamu

along with the sicknesses and sorrows,
wa'l-asqamu wa'l-ahzan.

and he will be blessed with bounty after his suffering and his pain,
wa yuna amu min ba'di bu'si-hi wa alami-hi

and he will be cured of his illness and his disease,
wa yusqa min maradi-hi wa suqmi-h.

so that all that he had to bear will cease to be.
hatta yazula ma bi-hi kana ma kan.

Here am I, a servant, a distant stranger, afflicted with misfortune.
wa ha ana'abdun na'in gharibun musabun

He is far away from his people and the homelands,
qad ba'uda'ani'l-ahli wa'l-awtan:

yet maybe this trouble and misery will leave him,
fa-'asa yazulu 'an-hu hadha't-ta'abu wa sh-shaqa:

and nearness and meeting will return to him,
wa ya'udu la-hu'l-qurbu wa'l-liqa:

and a mate and pure bliss will show themselves to him
wa yatara'a la-hu's-sal'u wa'n-naqa:

and the tamarisk and the ben-tree will appear for him,
wa yaluhu la-hu'l-athlu wa'l-ban:

and gracious favour and beneficence will come his way,
wa yanalu-hu'l-lutfu wa'l-ihsan:

and mercy and good pleasure will alight upon him.
wa tahullu'alai-hi'r-rahmatu wa'r-ridwan.

O Magnificent One, O Benefactor! O Generous One, O All-Merciful!
ya 'Azimu ya Mannan: ya Karimu ya Rahman.

O Owner of generosity and beneficence, and of mercy and forgiveness!
ya Sahiba'l-judi wa'l-ihsani wa'r-rahmati wa'l-ghufran.

O Allah, O Lord! O Allah, O Lord!
ya Allahu ya Rabb: ya Allahu ya Rabb:

O Allah, O Lord, have mercy on him who is oppressed by existing things,
ya Allahu ya Rabbu'rham man daqat 'alai-hi'l-akwan:

The two species [men and jinn] have not befriended him,
wa lam tu'nis-hu'th-thaqalan:

and he wanders in confusion by morning and night,
wa qad asbaha wa amsa muwallahan hairan:

and he finds himself a stranger,
wa adha ghariban

even though he may be among family and homelands;
wa law kana baina'l-ahli wa'l-awtan:

ill at ease, for no place gives him shelter;
munza'ijan la ya'wi-hi makan:

disturbed, for he is not relieved of his grief and sorrow
qaliqan la yulhi-hi'an baththi-hi wa huzni-hi

by the changing of the times;
taghayyuru'l-azman:

lonely, for his heart is not befriended by any human beings or jinn.
mustawhishan la ya'nasu qalbu-hu bi-insin wa la jann.

My Lord, is there in existence any lord apart from You,
Rabbi hal fi'l-wujudi rabbun siwa-ka

so that he may be called upon?
fa-yud'a

Or is there in the universe any god apart from You,
am hal fi'l-mamlakati ilahun ghairu-ka

so that hopes can be pinned on him?

fa-yurja.

Or is there any generous giver, other than You,
am hal karimun ghairu-ka fa-yutlaba min-hu'l-'ata.

so that gifts can be solicited from him?
fa-yutlaba min-hu'l-'ata.

Or is there any open-handed one, apart from You,
am hal thamma jawadun siwa-ka

so that grace and favour can be asked of him?
fa-yus'ala min-hu'l-fadlu wa'n-na'ma.

Or is there any judge, apart from You,
am hal hakimun ghairu-ka

so that complaints can be registered with him?
fa-turfa'a ilai-hi'sh-shakwa.

Or is there someone to whom the poor servant can be turned over?
am thamma man yuhalu'l-'abdu'l-faqiru'alai-h.

Or is there someone to whom the palms of the hands can be extended,
am hal thamma man tubsatu'l-akuffu

and to whom needs can be presented?
wa turfa'u'l-hajatu ilai-h.

There is nothing but Your generosity and Your munificence.
fa-laisa illa karamu-ka wa judu-ka

O He from whom there is no refuge except with Him!
ya man la malja'a min-hu illa ilai-h.

O He who affords protection, and against whom there is no protection!
ya man yujiru wa la yujaru'alai-h.

Is there any generous giver other than You, so that hope can be pinned on him?
a-hahuna karimun ghairu-ka fa-yurja

Or anyone apart from You, so that gifts can be asked of him?
am man siwa-ka jawadun fa-yus'ala min-hu'l-'ata.

My Lord, the friend has deserted me,
Rabbi qad jafa-ni'l-habib:

and the physician has lost patience with me,
wa malla-ni't-tabib:

and the enemy nearby has rejoiced at my affliction,
wa shamita biya'l-'uduwwu'l-qarib:

and grief and lamentation have shaken me severely.
wa'shtadda biya'l-karbu wa'n-nahib.

You are the Ever-Loving, the Ever-Near, the Kind, the Responsive One.
wa Anta'l-Wadudu'l-Qaribu'r-Ra'ufu'l-Mujib.

My Lord, to whom should I complain about my condition,
Rabbi ila man ashku halati

when You are the All-Knowing, the All-Capable?
wa Anta'l-'Alimu'l-Qadir:

Or of whom should I seek support,
am bi-man astansiru

when You are the Protecting Friend, the Supporter?
wa Anta'l-Waliyyu'n-Nasir.

Or of whom should I seek help,
am bi-man astaghithu

when You are the Protecting Friend, the Supervisor?
am bi-man astaghithu wa Anta'l-Waliyyu'n-Nazir:

Or with whom should I take refuge,
am ila man altaji'u

when You are the Generous Pardoner?
am ila man altaji'u wa Anta'l-Karimu's-Satir:

Or who is there to mend what I have broken,
am man dha'lladhi yajbaru kasri

when You are the Mender of hearts?
wa Anta li'l-qulubi Jabir:

Or who is there to forgive my serious sin,
am man dha'lladhi yaghfiru'azima dhanbi

when You are the All-Compassionate, the All-Forgiving?
wa Anta'r-Rahimu'l-Ghafiru

O Knower of what is within the innermost beings
Ya 'Aliman bi-ma fi's-sara'ir:

O He who is the Overseer of what is hidden in the cosnciences!
Ya man Huwa'l-Muttali'u'ala maknuni'd-dama'ir:

O He who is Prevailing over His servants!

Ya man Huwa fawqa'ibadi-hi Qahir:

O He who is the First, before all things, and the Last, after all things!
Ya man Huwa'l-Awwalu qabla kulli shai'in wa'l-Akhiru ba'da **kulli shai'.**

I ask You, O Lord of all things, because of Your power
as'alu-ka ya Rabba kulli shai'in bi-qudrati-ka

over all things, to forgive me for everything, so that You will **not question** me about anything.
hatta la tas'ala-ni'an shai'.

O He in whose Hand is the dominion of all things!
ya man bi-yadi-hi malakutu kulli shai'.

O He whom nothing can harm,
ya man la yadurru-hu shai'un

and whom nothing can benefit,
wa la yanfa'u-hu shai'un

and whom nothing can conquer,
wa la yaghlibu-hu shai'un .

and whom nothing can escape,
wa la ya'zubu'an-hu shai'un

and whom nothing can weary,
wa la ya'udu-hu shai'un

and who does not appeal to anything for help,
wa la yasta'inu bi-shai'in

and whom nothing can distract from anything,

wa la yashghalu-hu shai'un'an shai'in

and whom nothing resembles,
wa la yushbihu-hu shai'un

and whom nothing can disable.
wa la yu'jizu-hu shai'.

O He who is holding everything by the forelock,
ya man Huwa Akhidhun bi-nasiyati kulli shai'in

and in whose Hand are the keys to all things,
wa bi-yadi-hi maqalidu kulli

deflect from me the harmfulness of all things,
shai'ini'srif 'an-ni darra kulli shai'in

and make everything smooth for me,
wa sahhil li kulla shai'in

and do not call me to account for everything,
wa la tuhasib-ni bi-kulli shai'in

and bless me in everything,
wa barik li bi-kulli shai'in

and do not take me to task for everything,
wa la tu'akhidh-ni bi-kulli shai'in

and make everything easy for me,
wa yassir li kulla shai'in

and grant me everything,
wa hab li kulla shai'in

and give me the goodness of everything,

wa a'ti-ni khaira kulli shai'in

and protect me from the evil of everything.
wa'kfi-ni sharra kulli shai'.

O First of all things, and O Last of all things,
ya Awwala kulli shai'in wa ya Akhira kulli shai'in

and O Outer of all things, and O Inner of all things
wa ya Zahira kulli shai'in wa ya Batina kulli shai'in

and [He who is] above all things, and Reckoner of all things,
wa fawqa kulli shai'in wa Muhsiya kulli shai'in

and Originator of all things, and Restorer of all things,
wa Mubdi'a kulli shai'in wa Mu'ida kulli shai'in

and Knower of all things, and Encompasser of all things,
wa'Aliman bi-kulli shai'in wa Muhitan bi-kulli shai'in

and Seer of all things, and Witness over all things,
wa Basiran bi-kulli shai'in wa Shahidan'ala kulli shai'in

and Watcher over all things, and Gentle with all things,
wa Raqiban'ala kulli shai'in wa Latifan bi-kulli shai'in

and Aware of all things, and Inheritor of all things,
wa Khabiran bi-kulli shai'in wa Waritha kulli shai'in

and Controller of all things.
wa Qa'iman'ala kulli shai'.

O He in whose Hand is the dominion of all things,
ya man bi-yadi-hi malakutu kulli

forgive me for everything, for You are Capable of all things.
shai'ini'ghfir li kulla shai'in inna-ka'ala kulli shai'in Qadir.

O Allah, You are Safe from all things,
Allahumma inna-ka Aminun min kulli shai'in

and everything is afraid of You,
wa kullu shai'in kha'ifun min-ka

so, through Your security from all things and the fear of all things for You,
fa-bi-amni-ka min kulli shai'in wa khawfi kulli shai'in

forgive me for everything, so that You do not question me about anything.
min-ka'ghfir li kulla shai'in hatta la tas'ala-ni'an shai'.

O He in whose Hand is the dominion of all things,
ya man bi-yadi-hi malakutu kulli shai'in

You are indeed Capable of all things.
inna-ka'ala kulli shai'in Qadir.

O Allah, O Hope of the true believers,
Allahumma ya Raja'a'l-mu'minina

do not disappoint our hope.
la tukhayyib raja'a-na

O Helper of those who seek help, assist us!
wa ya Ghiyatha'l-mustaghithina aghthi-na

O Aide of the true believers, help us!
wa ya'Awna'l-mu'minina a'in-na

O Loving Friend of the penitent, relent toward us,

wa ya Habiba't-tawwabina tub'alai-na

and toward all Your servants who surrender [to Your will].
wa'ala'ibadi-ka'l-muslimina ajma'in.

In honour of the chief of the Messengers
bi-jahi sayyidi'l-Mursalina

and the seal of the Prophets, the trustworthy Chosen One,
wa khatami'n-Nabiyyina'l-Mustafa'l-Amini

the beloved of the Lord of All the Worlds.
habibi Rabbi'l-'alamin.

Amin, O Allah! Amin, O Lord of All the Worlds!
Amin. Allahumma Amin. ya Rabba'l-'alamin.

Allah and His angels shower blessings on the Prophet.
inna'llaha wa mala'ikata-hu yusalluna'ala'n-Nabiyy :

O you who truly believe, invoke blessings upon him
ya ayyuha'lladhina amanu sallu 'alai-hi

and salute him with a worthy salutation.
wa sallimu taslima. (33:56)

O Allah, grant blessing and peace and grace to our master Muhammad,
Allahumma salli wa sallim wa barik 'ala sayyidi-na Muhammadin

and to his family and his Companions, one and all.
wa'ala ali-hi wa sahbi-hi ajma'in.

Glory be to your Lord, the Lord of Majesty,

subhana Rabbi-ka Rabbi'l-'Izzati

far from what they attribute!
'amma yasifun.

And peace be upon those sent as Messengers!
wa salamun'ala'l-Mursalin.

And praise be to Allah, Lord of the Worlds!
wa'l-hamdu li'llahi Rabbi'l-'alamin. (37:180-83)

*****

RIJAL AL-GHAIB
THE MANNER OF SHAIKH 'ABD AL-QADIR'S SALUTATION [SALAM]
(May Allah sanctify his innermost being)
to the men of the Unseen [rijal al-Ghaib]
(Sanctified be their innermost beings).

In the Name of Allah, the All-Merciful, the All-Compassionate.
Bismi'llahi'r-Rahmani'r-Rahim.

Peace be upon you, O men of the Unseen!
as-salamu'alai-kum ya rijala'l-Ghaib.

Peace be upon you, O sanctified spirits!
as-salamu'alai-kum ya ayyuha'l-arwahu'l-mutaqaddasa.

O presidents, O noblemen, O overseers, O spiritual deputies!
ya nuqaba ya nujaba ya ruqaba ya budala

O mainstays of the earth, four mainstays! O two leaders!
ya awtada'l-ardi awtadun arba'a: ya imaman:

O Cardinal Pole! O matchless individual! O trustees!

ya Qutbu ya fardu ya umana':

Provide me with assistance, look on me with favour,
aghithu-ni bi-ghawthatin wa'nDuru-ni bi-naDratin

treat me with compassion, fulfil my wish and my objective,
wa'rhamu-ni wa hassilu muradi wa maqsudi

and attend to the satisfaction of my needs,
wa qumu'ala qada'i hawa'iji

in the presence of our Prophet Muhammad
'inda Nabiyyi-na Muhammadin

(Allah bless him and give him peace).
(salla'llahu 'alai-hi wa sallam).

May Allah (Exalted is He) grant you peace in this world and the Hereafter.
sallama-kumu'llahu (ta'ala) fi'd-dunya wa'l-akhira.

O Allah, bestow blessings on al-Khidr!
Allahumma salli ala'l-Khidr.

WIRD LI-DHAHAB AT-TA'AB
[LITANY FOR RELIEF FROM WEARINESS]

One of the subtle offerings [daqa'iq] of Shaikh 'Abd al-Qadir (may Allah sanctify his innermost being) is the supplication for relief from weariness [dhahab at-ta'ab] and for the traversing [lit., "folding up"] of the earth [tayy al-ard]. It is appropriate for someone who can recite with a sound heart, a truthful intention, and a strong sense of direction, as well as a bond of connection. It reads as follows:

In the Name of Allah, the All-Merciful, the All-Compassionate.
Bismi'llahi'r-Rahmani'r-Rahim

"In the Name of Allah" be upon my heart,
Bismi'llahi'ala qalbi

until its thirst is quenched.
hatta yurwa

"In the Name of Allah" be upon my knees,
Bismi'llahi'ala rukabi

until they grow strong.
hatta taqwa

"In the Name of Allah" be upon the earth,
Bismi'llahi ala'l-ardi

until it is travelled over [lit., "rolled up"].
hatta tutwa.

HIZB AN-NASR - 1
[THE RECITAL OF VICTORY BY SHAIKH 'ABD AL-QADIR]
(sanctified be his innermost being).

In the Name of Allah, the All-Merciful, the All-Compassionate.
Bismi'llahi'r-Rahmani'r-Rahim.

O Allah, O He Whom the eyes do not see,
Allahumma ya Man la tara-hu'l-'uyun:

and with Whom mere suppositions do not blend,
wa la tukhalitu-hu'D-Dunun:

and Whom the portrayers do not portray,

wa la yasifu-hu'l-wasifun:

and Who does not fear misfortunes,
wa la yakhafu'd-dawa'ir:

and Who is not destroyed by dire consequences.
wa la tufni-hi'l-'awaqib.

He knows the weights of the mountains,
ya'lamu mathaqila'l-jibali

and the measures of the oceans,
wa maka'ila'l-bihar:

and the number of the drops of rain,
wa'adada qatri'l-amtar:

and the number of the leaves on the trees,
wa'adada waraqi'l-ashjar:

and the number of the things on which the night casts darkness,
wa 'adada ma adlama 'alai-hi'l-lailu

and on which the day sheds light.
wa ashraqa'alai-hi'n-nahar.

Not one of the heavens is concealed from Him, nor any earth,
wa la tuwari min-hu sama'un min sama'in wa la ardun min ardin

nor any mountain, without His knowing what is in its very depth,
wa la jibalun illa ya'lamu ma fi qa'ri-ha

and the heavens and the earth are in submission to His Majesty.
wa fi'stikanati'ADamati-hi's-samawatu wa'l-ardu

O Allah, let the best of my work be its final results,
Allahumma'j 'al khaira 'amali khawatima-hu

and let the best of my days be the day on which I meet with You.
wa khaira ayyami yawma alqa-ka fi-h:

You are indeed Capable of all things.
inna-ka'ala kulli shai'in Qadir.

O Allah, if someone is hostile toward me, treat him with hostility.
Allahumma man 'ada-ni fa-'adi-h:

If someone deceives me, deceive him.
wa man kada-ni fa-kid-h:

If someone puts my life in danger, destroy him.
wa man bagha'alayya bi-mahlakatin fa-ahlik-h:

If someone sets a trap for me, grab hold of him.
wa man nasaba li fakhkhan fa-khudh-h.

Extinguish for me the fire of him who kindles his fire to harm me,
wa atfi 'an-ni nara man shabba nara-hu 'alayya

and protect me from what distresses me
wa'kfi-ni ma ahamma-ni

in the business of this world and the Hereafter,

min amri'd-dunya wa'l-akhirati

and confirm my hope with realization.
wa saddiq raja'i bi't-tahqiq.

O Tender One! O Gentle One!
ya Shafiqu ya Rafiq:

Relieve me of every hardship,
farrij'an-ni kulla diq:

and do not burden me with what I cannot bear.
wa la tuhammil-ni ma la utiq:

You are indeed the Worthy Sovereign!
inna-ka Anta'l-Maliku'l-Haqiq.

O Radiant Source of the Proof!
ya Mushriqa'l-Burhan:

O He of Whom no place is empty, protect me
ya Man la yakhlu min-hu makanuni'hrus-ni

with Your eye that never sleeps,
bi-'aini-ka'llati la tanam:

and shield me with Your shelter
wa'knuf-ni bi-kanafi-ka

and Your pillar, which can never be dislodged.
wa rukni-ka'lladhi la yuram

My heart is now fully convinced that there is no god but You,
inna-hu qad tayaqqana qalbi inna-ka la ilaha illa Anta

and that I shall not perish while You are with me.

wa inni la ahliku wa Anta ma'i.

O All-Merciful One, treat me mercifully with Your power over me!
ya Rahmanu fa-'rham-ni bi-qudrati-ka 'alayya.

O Splendid One, looked to in hope by every splendid being!
ya 'Adiman yurja li-kulli 'adim:

O All-Knowing One, O All-Forbearing One!
Ya 'Alimu ya Halim:

You are Aware of my condition,
wa Anta bi-hali 'Alim:

and Capable of my salvation, and that is easy for You,
wa'ala khalasi Qadir: wa huwa 'alai-ka yasir:

so treat me with gracious favour in Your judgment.
fa-'mnun 'alayya bi-qada'i-k.

O Most Noble of the most noble,
ya Akrama'l-akramina

and O Most Generous of the most generous,
wa ya Ajwada'l-ajwadina

and O Swiftest of the reckoners!
wa ya Asra'a'l-hasibin.

O Lord of All the Worlds and O Most Merciful of the merciful!
ya Rabba'l-'alamina wa ya Arhama'l-arhamin.

O Allah, do not make my life a misery,
Allahumma la taj'al li-'aishi kadda:

and do not cause my plea to be rejected.
wa la li-du'a'i radda:

Do not make me a servant to anyone but You,
wa la taj'al-ni li-ghairi-ka 'abda:

and do not plant love in my heart for anything other than You,
wa la taj'al fi qalbi li-siwa-ka wudda:

for I do not say that You have any counterpart,
fa-inni la aqulu la-ka diddan

or any partner or any rival.
wa la sharikan wa la nidda.

You are indeed Capable of all things,
inna-ka'ala kulli shai'in Qadir.

and there is no power nor any strength
wa la hawla wa la quwwata

except with Allah, the All-High, the Almighty.
illa bi'llahi'l-'Aliyyi'l-'Adim.

May Allah bless our master Muhammad and his family
wa salla'llahu 'ala sayyidi-na Muhammadin wa'ala ali-hi

and his Companions, and may He grant them peace
wa sahbi-hi wa sallama tasliman

in great abundance until the Day of Reckoning.
kathiran ila Yawmi'd-Din.

Amin.

HIZB AN-NASR - 2
ANOTHER RECITAL OF VICTORY [HIZB AN-NASR]
by Shaikh 'Abd al-Qadir
(Sanctified be his innermost being).

In the Name of Allah, the All-Merciful, the All-Compassionate.
Bismi'llahi'r-Rahmani'r-Rahim.

O Allah, I beg You to grant me immersion in the ocean of the light
Allahumma as 'alu-ka ghamsatan fi bahri nuri

of Your compelling Dignity, outwardly and inwardly potent and powerful,
Haibati-ka'l-qahirati'D-Dahirati'l-batinati'l-qadirati'l-muqtadira:

until my face is aglow with rays from the light of Your Dignity.
hatta yatala'la'a wajhi bi-shu'a'atin min nuri Haibati-k.

It will dazzle the eyes of the envious, the rebellious and the devils,
Takhtafu 'uyuna'l-hasadati wa'l-maradati wa'sh-shayatin:

among all of mankind and the jinn,
mina'l-insi wa'l-jinni ajma'in:

so they cannot strike me with the arrows of their envy,
fa-la yarshuqu-ni bi-sihami hasadi-him

and with their inner and outer intrigues,
wa maka'idi-hum'l-batinati wa'd-Dahirati

and so their eyes are ashamed to look at me,

wa tasiru absaru-hum khashi'atan li-ru'yati

and their necks are bowed before my onslaught.
wa riqabu-hum khadi'atan li-satwati.

Shield me, O Allah, with the shield of which
wa'hjub-ni Allahumma bi'l-hijabi'lladhi

the inner side is radiant light, so that my spiritual states
batinu-hu'n-nuru

are beautified by its intimate friendship,
fa-tabtahiju ahwali bi-unsi-hi

and my words and my deeds are fortified by its touch,
wa tata 'ayyadu aqwali wa af 'ali bi-hissi-hi

and of which the outer side is fire,
wa Dahiru-hu'n-naru

so that it scorches the faces of my foes
fa-talfahu wujuha a'da'i

with a scorching that cuts their desires off from me,
lafhatan taqta'u mawadda-hum'an-ni

until they turn away from their objectives, as outcasts,
hatta tusaddu'an mawaridi-him khasi'ina

losers and failures, disgraced and abased and humiliated.
khasirina khashi'ina khadi'ina mutadhallilina

They will turn their backs and lay waste to the lands,
yuwalluna'l-adbara wa yukharribuna'd-diyara

and ruin their homes with their own hands

wa yukharribuna buyuta-hum bi-aidi-him

and the hands of the believers.
wa aidi'l-mu'minin.

I also beg You for the light that acts as a shield
wa as'alu-ka'n-nura'lladhi'htajaba bi-hi

for the preservation of the honour of the lights
qiwamu namusi anwari

of Your Countenance, the light by which You are shielded
Wajhi-ka'n-nura'lladhi'htajabta bi-hi

from the perception of the eyes.
'an idraki'l-absar.

[I beg You] to shield me with the lights of Your Names,
an tahjuba-ni bi-anwari Asma'i-ka

within the lights of Your Secrets,
fi anwari Asrari-ka

with a shield thick enough to defend me against every deficiency
hijaban kathifan yadfa'u 'an-ni kulla naqsin

that might affect me in my essential and my incidental nature,
yukhalitu-ni fi jawhariyyati wa fi 'aradiyyati

and which will form a barrier between me
wa yahulu baini

and anyone who seeks to do me harm,
wa baina man arada-ni bi-su'.

[I beg You for] that by which You will revitalize me,
wa ma tuhyi-ni bi-hi

from among Your gracious favours which You have bestowed,
min fada'il-ka'llati manahta bi-ha

and Your excellent bounties in which You have inundated me.
wa fawadili-ka'llati ghamarta-ni fi-ha.

[I beg You for] whatever is assigned to me,
wa ma ilayya

and incumbent upon me, and due to me, and for me,
wa'alayya wa bi wa li

and about me, and in my interest,
wa'an-ni wa fiyya.

for You are the Repeller of everything evil and despicable,
fa-inna-ka Dafi'u kulli su'in wa makruh:

and You are Capable of all things.
wa Anta 'ala kulli sha'in Qadir.

O Shining Source of every light, clothe me from Your Light
ya Munawwira kulli nurin albis-ni min Nuri-ka

in clothing that illuminates for me whatever I find confusing
libasan yudihu li ma'ltabasa 'alayya

among my inner and outer states of being.
mina ahwali'l-batinati wa'd-Dahira:

Extinguish the lights of my enemies and my enviers,
wa'tmis anwara a'da'i wa hussadi

so that they cannot approach me except in abject humiliation,
hatta la yahtadu ilayya illa bi'dh-dhulli

in submission and ruination and exhaustion,
wa'l-inqiyadi wa'l-halakati wa'n-nafadi

since no despotic oppressive, overbearing relic of them will remain.
fa-la tubqi min-hum baqiyatan baghiyatan taghiyatan 'atiya.

Let the guards of Hell restrain them from me,
aqmi'-hum 'an-ni bi'z-zabaniya:

and let their pillars be demolished by the angels eight in number,
wa hudda arkana-hum bi'l-mala'ikati'th-thamaniya:

and seize them by every forelock,
wa khudh-hum min kulli nasiya:

for the sake of each Name by which You have named Yourself,
bi-haqqi kulli'smin huwa la-ka sammaita bi-hi Nafsa-ka

or have revealed in Your Book,
aw anzalta-hu fi Kitabi-ka

or have made known to one of Your creatures,
aw 'allamta-hu ahadan min khalqi-ka

or have kept in Your presence within the knowledge of the Unseen,
awi'sta'tharta bi-hi fi 'ilmi'l-Ghaibi 'inda-ka

and for the sake of that which is Yours by right,
wa bi-haqqi-ka 'alai-ka

and that which You owe to every owner of a rightful claim on You.
wa bi-haqqi-ka 'ala kulli dhi haqqin 'alai-k.

O Truth, O Clearly Manifest, O Ever-Living, O Self-Sustaining One!
ya Haqqu ya Mubinu ya Hayyu ya Qayyum:

O Allah! O Lord! O Source of Help!
ya Allahu ya Rabbahu ya Ghiyathah.

I beseech You by Your most beautiful Names,
As 'alu-ka bi-Asma'ika'l-husna

and by Your most high and perfect Attributes,
wa bi-Sifati-ka't-tammati'l-'ulya

and by Your most exalted Dignity,
bi-'Arshi-ka wa ma hawa

and by Your Throne and what it contains,
wa bi-Jaddi-ka'l-a'la wa

and by Him who established Himself upon the Throne,
wa bi-Man 'ala'l-'Arshi'stawa

and encompassed the sovereignty,
wa 'ala'l-mulki'htawa

and by him who drew near and came down,
dana fa-tadalla

till he was two bows' length or nearer.
fa-kana qaba qawsaini aw adna. (53:8,9)

[I beg You] to let the sun of awesome splendour, overwhelming,
an tutli'a shamsa'l-haibati'l-qahirati'l-

brilliant, outwardly and inwardly potent and powerful,
bahirati'd-Dahirati'l-qadirati'l-muqtadirati

shine upon my face, so that blindness will afflict any person
'ala wajhi hatta ya'ma kullu shakhsin

who stares at me with the eye of enmity, scorn and contempt.
yanduru ilayya bi-'aini'l-'adawati wa'l-izdira'i wa'l-istihza':

It will turn him away when he approaches me, repelled by the
fa-tudbiru-hu'inda iqbali-hi ilayya mustaraddan

devastating perils and the threatening disasters,
bi'l-makhawifi'l-muhlikati wa'l-bawa'iqi'l-mudrika.

Your embrace of all things will thus embrace them,
fa-tuhitu bi-him ihatatu-ka bi-kulli shai'in

until not a remnant of them remains,
hatta la tubqiya min-hum baqiyatan

and they find no protection against it.
wa la yajidu min-ha waqiya.

"In the Name of Allah" be in front of us.
Bismi'llahi min quddami-na

"In the Name of Allah" be behind us.
Bismi'llahi min wara'i-na

"In the Name of Allah" be above us.

Bismi'llahi min fawqi-na

"In the Name of Allah" be beneath us.
Bismi'llahi min tahti-na

"In the Name of Allah" be on our right.
Bismi'llahi 'an aimani-na

"In the Name of Allah" be on our left.
Bismi'llahi 'an shama'ili-na

O our Master! O our Patron!
ya Sayyida-na ya Mawla-na

Answer our supplication and grant us our request!
fa-'stajib du'a-na wa a'ti-na su'la-na

So of the people who did wrong the last remnant was cut off.
fa-quti'a dabiru'l-qawmi'lladhina Dalamu :

Praise be to Allah, Lord of All the Worlds!
wa'l-hamdu li'llahi Rabbi'l-'alamin. (6:45)

And Allah is behind them, Encompassing.
wa'llahu min wara'i-him Muhit.

Nay, but it is a glorious Qur'an, on a Treasured Tablet.
bal huwa Qur'anun majid: fi Lawhin Mahfud. (85:20–22)

If We will, We can send down on them from the sky a sign
in nasha' nunazzil 'alai-him mina's-sama'i ayatan

so that their necks would remain bowed before it.
fa-dallat a'naqu-hum la-ha khadi'in. (26:4)

And praise be to Allah, the Lord of All the Worlds.

va'l-hamdu li'llahi Rabbi'l-'alamin.

In the Name of Allah, the All-Merciful, the All-Compassionate
Bismi'llahi'r-Rahmani'r-Rahim

O Allah! O All-Merciful, O All-Compassionate One!
ya Allahu ya Rahmanu ya Rahim:

O Ever-Living, O Eternally Self-Sustaining One!
ya Hayyu ya Qayyum.

Kaf-Ha-Ya'-'Ain-Sad. (19:1)

O Loving One, O Source of Help!
ya Wadudu ya Musta'anu

Ha-Mim. 'Ain-Sin-Qaf. (42:1,2)

May Allah bless our master Muhammad and his family
wa salla'llahu 'ala sayyidi-na Muhammadin wa 'ala ali-hi

and his Companions, and may He grant them peace.
wa sahbi-hi wa sallam.

*****